To Die and to Live

Paul S. Minear

TO DIE
AND TO LIVE

*Christ's Resurrection
and Christian Vocation*

A Crossroad Book

THE SEABURY PRESS · NEW YORK

To
five children who are grand
in more ways than one

Robert
Edward
Elisabeth
William
Michael

1977
The Seabury Press
815 Second Avenue
New York, N.Y. 10017

Library of Congress Cataloging in Publication Data

Minear, Paul Sevier, 1906–
To die and to live.
"A Crossroad book."
Includes bibliographical references and index.
    1. Jesus Christ—Resurrection.   2. Vocation.
I. Title.
BT481.M56   232.9′7   77–8238
ISBN 0–8164–0340–6

Contents

2988

Acknowledgments

The final drafting of this book has released memories of personal associations that emerged during the earlier stages of its preparation. Many persons have contributed to my thinking on this subject, in ways and at depths which I cannot recapture or reduce to printed words. I must therefore be content simply to indicate the major occasions on which those contributions were made: meetings with faculty and students at Minnesota State College in St. Cloud; a summer conference of campus ministers held at Duke University; classes in the 1976 summer session at the Vancouver School of Theology; a retreat for ministers from United Church of Christ parishes in Maine; the 1976 Convocation at the North Park Theological Seminary in Chicago, where four chapters were presented as the Nils W. Lund Memorial Lectures. To these hosts and audiences I extend cordial greetings and sincere gratitude.

The source of various ideas and quotations will, I trust, be adequately recognized by notes. In the case of three authors, I wish to clarify possible misunderstandings. In the last chapter I make extensive use of a pattern of analysis advanced in Paul Ricoeur's *Symbolism of Evil.* I wish to say that in this case my ways of intepreting the symbolisms of "archaeology, teleology, and eschatology" had taken shape before I found welcome support in his study. Likewise, in Chapter 5 the distinction I draw between disciples at first hand and those at second hand is strikingly similar to the discussion in Søren Kierkegaard's *Philosophical Fragments;* again my composition of this chapter preceded my discovery of that similarity. This is not said, of course, to deny or to deplore my indebtedness at other points to the great Danish exegete. Finally, in Chapter 1, I refer to some germinal ideas of Richard Kroner; in this case the references fall far short of doing justice to the continuing influence and inspiration of this wise friend of many years.

PART I
A Thought Experiment

Whoever can give his people better stories than the ones they live in is like the priest in whose hands common bread and wine become capable of feeding the very soul. [1]

1
The Heart's Horizons

to pierce the heart's residuum
. . . And there to find music for a single line,
Equal to memory, one line in which
The vital music formulates the words. [1]

A Refugee

This is the century of the refugee. Nothing is more typical of our time than the anxious flight and the turbulent resettlement of millions of footsore exiles. The catalog of peoples who have recently been "displaced" seems endless: East Germans, Czechs, Hungarians, Latvians, Pakistani, Poles, Congolese, Bengali, Cambodians, Vietnamese, Angolans, Portuguese, Palestinians, Kurds, Chileans. . . . No continent has been spared, no nation is immune. In fact the most traumatic migrations may take place within the boundaries of a single nation.

Nor can we exclude from this sad roster millions who have continued to live in the same city, but who have lost contact with their ancestral communities. No longer can they call any space or any time their very own. They no longer belong anywhere. Homeless, the center of their world is located wherever they happen to be at the moment. Who can probe the wounds inflicted by such rootlessness? Who can prescribe a healing ointment for those wounds?

But why do we speak of refugees only in the third person, "they"? In our deepest selves we know that all of us are refugees of a sort. Like the nomad Tuaregs of the Sahel, we roam desolate sands, hoping desperately that an oasis will appear on the horizon. All our living is done *pro tem;* in every profession mobility has become a prime requirement. All our thoughts and activities are infected by a readiness to burn the bridge we have just crossed. Is such a self-image too melodramatic? Perhaps. But let those who do not feel the earthquake tremors count themselves fortunate. Or are they only self-deceived? Be that as it may, we are all actual or potential refugees, distinguished only by degrees of readiness to meet the next crisis. Whenever we encounter homeless wanderers, they remind us of our own vulnerability; and this fact gives awesome metaphorical weight to the term *refugee.* In an earlier century the picture of the pilgrim had become one of the most evocative images. Today the term *refugee* has absorbed many nuances from that earlier parable of human existence. The stories that most of us "live in" are the stories of the hurried flight of exiles rather than the patient quest of pilgrims. Even so, certain features of the pilgrim parable remain relevant to the current situation.

Few pictures are more ancient, more archetypal, than the picture of the pilgrim. None better expresses inner restlessness and outer uncertainty, the sense of continual movement and the ache of fatigue. A pilgrim is incomplete without his packsack into which is stuffed whatever is most precious, most essential. In comparison with all one's possessions, the backpack is a pathetic pittance; but without it a person would be forlorn indeed. Each day, the pilgrim must ask again: what am I able to take along? what must I take? So whenever we think of ourselves as pilgrims, we begin instinctively to choose and to reject, to weigh and to measure, whatever is to go with us.

The analogy of the packsack invites a bit of reflection. It is the pilgrim's link to the life being left behind; it makes available for today's hunger whatever has accrued from previous experience. The whole of that experience trudges along the same path; memories, whether cloudy or clear, of people and places, of trophies and defeats. These memories, which belong to no other traveler, bestow an identity as distinctive as fingerprints. A packsack may be laid aside at will, but not those prints. They form a private autobiography, more inclusive and more accurate than any written volume could be.

How does an autobiography grow? Perhaps the question is too simple to require an answer. It grows whenever a person adds today's experience to his previous ones. Each fresh happening becomes assimilated into the totality of reminiscence. If it is like other experiences it will be filed away in the same pigeonhole of memory; if it is wholly novel a new pigeonhole may be created for it, or it may be dismissed. The degree of similarity determines the ease of assimilation. But whether easy or difficult, each fragment of the story becomes incorporated into the whole story. A traveler lives with his entire autobiography; each day he adds something to it. The longer he lives the more it will become true that everything that happens will remind him of something else, and the more he will come to rely on the inner continuities of that story. Each memory will derive its significance from the total fund of memories. The smoothness of his assimilation will be an index to his health, a health threatened by various types of anarchy but strengthened by the absorption of each fresh episode into the story as a whole.[2]

We can learn much about this process of absorption by observing three kinds of situations in which the process is broken off. The first is that dread disease known as amnesia. Nothing else so quickly or so radically shows how completely a person depends on his memory for a sense of identity and direction. When all recollections of the past are blocked out, a terrifying vacuum is created at the very center of things. Death is not too sharp a word to describe this total tearing loose from the fabric of normal human associations. Second is that form of senility wryly called one's "anecdotage," when memories of the distant past smother more recent recollections. Nostalgia takes over. Now only the photographs and clippings in the worn and treasured album can arouse interest; what happens today has no power to stimulate either enjoyment or anticipation. In effect, the autobiography is complete

except for the date of the obituary. The third disease is that
to which Alvin Toffler has bequeathed the name "future
shock." In this situation a person encounters changes so rapid
and so extreme that they can no longer be absorbed into
working memory. When one meets too many strangers, all
people become anonymous. So many bizarre sounds bombard
the ears that they lose the ability to distinguish whisper from
tornado. A person can no longer find himself in the whirling
kaleidoscope of news bulletins. Amnesia, senility, future shock
—these three diseases of the memory prove how essential it is
to be able to relate smoothly each successive fragment of experience to the totality of consciousness.

We must not, however, forget that a pilgrim's backpack contains much more than recollections. It is also filled with hopes,
however tenuous, for what lies ahead. From his anticipations
the pilgrim derives whatever energy may be needed for trudg-
ing the next mile. Without some specific goal there would be
no forward or backward, no reason to move on, nothing to do
but to sit "waiting for Godot." Hazards can be endured and
hardships accepted if some destination lies ahead; but when
tomorrow dies, courage evaporates. One's hopes, together
with memories, enable him to relate today's round to the
whole of experience. Each milepost reminds the traveler again
of both origin and destination. It is these two realities that
enable a person to calculate distances, to answer such insistent
questions as where, when, why.

> Man possesses himself, disposes of himself, understands him-
> self in and by the anamnesis by which he retains the past and
> the prognosis by which he lays hold of what is to come.[3]

Disease may strike the pilgrim's hopes in much the same way
that it affects his memory. Corresponding to amnesia, a forget-
fulness of the future may prevail, when every day becomes
gray because neither fear nor anticipation of the morrow can
be felt. The results may be less instantaneous, less dramatic
than in the case of amnesia, for the sense of identity does

remain partially intact and a certain momentum keeps moving us forward, from waking to sleeping to waking. Yet the end results are no less devastating, for hopeless existence is hell. Paralleling that disease of memory which we have called senility is a disease of hope in which the future serves only as an escape from the present. And because the near future provides only a temporary escape, this diseased hope becomes infatuated with a distant future. The more distant the future, the more effective the escape. The more distant the future, the more undisciplined our dreams, until at last, drunk on dreams, we allow an impossible but alluring future to blot out the intolerable present. The goal may now be clear, but it is so remote that no milepost brings us appreciably closer to it. Finally, future shock has its twin in a diseased imagination that dabbles in so many contradictory expectations that we either postpone all choosing or choose a glut of goals, none of which can survive the next day's turbulence. Tomorrow's zig follows today's zag. These diseases destroy the possibility of developing any inner relation between now and always. Life has no weft left to hold its warp.[4]

Every person who reflects on experience will surely recall struggling with one or another of these diseases of memory and hope. If he has been able to develop inner stamina it will have come by way of a series of victories over these maladies, victories never to be taken for granted, inasmuch as no permanent immunity is possible. In fact, the odds against the pilgrim are so great that each victory becomes something of a mystery and a miracle.

Paralleling the maladies just described are many factors conducive to health. Among them, not the least potent, is a reality to which we point when we use the word *vocation.*[5] The sense of vocation, of being singled out or called, gives a person a point of origin around which his memories can coalesce, a destination that can include all expectations, and a set of priorities that enables him to order his conflicting desires. Vocation is relevant simultaneously to each fragment of experience and to the totality of experience.[6] It connotes an identity conferred on a person and accepted by that person as his own. It suggests an initiative from an invisible source outside the private stock of desires, and inner demands from within the deepest springs of being. Of course we all find it difficult to describe in precise detail either that initiative or our response to it. The words may be as vague as those of Dag Hammerskjold, "I did answer Yes to Someone—or Something,"[7] or they may be as diamond-sharp as those of the apostle Paul: "When he who had set me apart before I was born, and had called me through his grace, was pleased to reveal his son to me . . ." (Gal. 1:11–24). In either case it is only when this sense of vocation dies that the diseases of memory or of hope can thrive; the stronger the sense of vocation, the greater the spiritual stamina. Vocation is no esoteric matter, important to only a few extraordinary individuals; it is an everyday source of energy that determines the health of all. Ordinarily it is less like a bolt of lightning than like a daily sunrise.

> Out of the primeval chaos of sleep he calls me to be a life again. Out of the labyrinth of selves, born and unborn, remembered and forgotten, he calls me to be a self again, a single, true, whole self. He calls me to be this rather than that; he calls me to be here rather than there; he calls me to be now rather than then. He calls me to be of all things me, as this morning when the alarm went off and the children came in or your dream woke you, he called you to be of all things you.[8]

In the following chapters we will return constantly to this matter of vocation, and to the ways in which it provides us with both map and compass.

A normal way for a pilgrim to record what is happening is by telling a story, in which the subject of many sentences will be "I." Other people will, of course, enter, but they will win their place by their contacts with that "I." If he thinks at all, each pilgrim will make daily entries in the diary of his mind. The existence of this diary reflects the feeling that what happens can and should be remembered. Some significance, however minuscule, inheres in each event as well as in the total sequence of events. To consult that diary is one way of becoming aware of the links that bind this immediate segment of life to the total span. Such consultation often provides the best clue to the actual vocation of the diarist.

Although it is by no means a common or necessary thing, some travelers commit their diary to writing, a process that forces them to a higher degree of self-consciousness concerning otherwise trivial happenings. Then, by rereading previous entries, they learn much which otherwise would have been squandered—lessons about the transience of some things that seemed permanent, the permanence of some things that seemed transient, and the fluctuating strength of specific memories and hopes. They recall intentions that have evaporated under the pressures of living or that have been reinforced by those pressures. Each recollection of the story as a whole makes it a new story, a new version that embodies the most recent experiences. Any introduction of new characters affects the drama, as does any changing of the stage setting. As Wallace Stevens has written, "We live in the description of a place, and not the place itself."[9] It is that description that changes every time we consult the diary. But, through all the changes, something will remain the same, and that something provides the diarist with important clues to both his intended vocation and his actual vocation. Whatever it is that links one episode to the others will point to a pattern, a unity, the realization or frustration of a calling, not necessarily conscious and usually not of the pilgrim's own concoction. This thread that links disparate occasions into a single continuous skein may be of little interest to others, but it will be of primary concern to the diarist. It will reveal to him some intimations of the hidden beginnings and endings of his own journey and of the energies that impel him forward. The word *vocation* is a pointer to that mystery, providing the inner links between the moment and the momentous. The achievement of clear comprehension of that mystery is nothing short of miraculous.

Why miraculous? Because of the vast odds against such comprehension and such coherence, and because at every stage the story moves from one conflict and crisis to another. The clock and the calendar seem to conspire to prevent such a miracle. Each autobiography is interrupted, as well as punctuated, by time.

> *Time is your barracks and your discipline.*
> *Heart-ticking clocks, bugles and bells that chime*
> *Irrevocable sequence now begin*
> *Through night and day and night and day and night*
> *Their quick partition of the infinite.*
> *. . . . .*
> *Your every breath's a nickel or a dime*
> *Budgeted and audited by time.* [10]

Yet each person's autobiography activates a partial freedom from the time clock and the referee's whistle. Memory thumbs its nose at the purely mechanical rhythms of the calendar. Hope evokes and even requires a limited freedom from times and places. If routine is essential, so also is liberation from routine. The heart is eager to follow the poet's injunction:

> *Watch your thoughts, and leap for the delightful*
> *Occasion (it will occur) that is not time,*
> *When contemplation's dragons are not frightful,*
> *And a bright interruption of time's scheme*
> *Will show a glimpse of what lost Adam knew*
> *Before the devil turned his heart askew;* [11]

So, too, each person's story discloses both how he is limited by the spaces where he lives and how he breaks through those limits. Each "here" (for example, a prison cell) exerts its power to restrict movement, but each act of memory and hope celebrates a victory over such restriction. If one doubts it, let him open his eyes to what is happening in the departure and arrival lobbies at any airport. Or let him read the letters and diaries of people in prison. When I listen alertly to another person, the conversation produces a fusion of horizons, in which the other's space and time coalesce with mine and mine with his. When I relate my experience in today's space to my experience in all the places of my pilgrimage and when I include within my story all those places which belong to the story of those whom I love, then each day's space is enlarged to include many epochs and worlds. Without a story that has cohered around a continuing sense of vocation, the promise of liberation to this wider world is eliminated.

We should not underestimate the degree to which this coherence has disappeared from contemporary life. Two book reviews on the same page of a recent newspaper remind us of this loss. Speaking of recent novels as a group, George Stade writes:

> Contemporary reality . . . is a chaos of disconnections, a blizzard of noise . . . voices on telephones, intercoms, radios, TV, movie sound tracks; the slang of school children and hipsters; the double quackduckspeak of commissars of law, science, business, PR and education; the broken poetry of drunkenness and nervous breakdown—all interrupting each other.[12]

Roger Shattuck writes:

> The music, you suddenly realize, has stopped. You cannot remember when it happened. All you can hear now is what sounds like comic efforts to articulate the silence. No one will play a tune any more. Nor will anyone tell a proper story. We must be satisfied with episodes, anecdotes, jokes, games. For we have learned that there is no beginning and no end.[13]

Within that "blizzard of noise" can any person's story retain its coherence? Only by a miracle. Within that blizzard any notion of a compelling vocation becomes a mirage. Yet an occasional poet refuses to accept such a fate:

> *We come alone out of the dust*
> *We go alone back to the dust;*
> *But in between the black and black*
> *We have the universe for track;*

For seventy years the air is ours,
The wide sky and the crowded flowers,
And more than contemplation should
Justify our livelihood;[14]

It is not, of course, the external cacophonies alone that destroy the sense of vocation; internal struggles can also be as destructive, when passions and ambitions are not disciplined and ordered. A person remembers—yes, but his memories may cover the careers of a dozen Dr. Jekylls and a dozen Mr. Hydes within himself. He hopes, but those hopes may shift with amazing speed and incredible unpredictability. If he keeps a diary, the self who composed the entry in August may bear little similarity to the self who made another entry in December. *One* story? No, many. *One* vocation? How fantastic. The deepest problem is not the drowning of an individual in the ocean of humanity, not the dwarfing of his little acre by the whole globe, nor the vanishing of his day in geological eons, nor the triviality of what happens between dawn and dusk. Rather it is the kaleidoscopic shift of multiple selves that makes it absurd to speak of a single story or a single vocation. Before that absurdity can be overcome, before one can speak cogently of linking one fragment of experience to total experience, there must be a series of miraculous victories by which each self becomes in fact a single self.

The road to those victories is marked by crucial struggles between one vocation and a host of competitors. Each calling competes with others for the day's allegiance. The competition varies according to stages in the life cycle: childhood, adolescence, college days, choice of profession, middle age. Competition among callings is often a function of the different worlds in which a person lives: the office or shop, the home, the place of play, the voluntary associations. Each of these worlds sows its own seed and expects to garner its own harvest. Each community to which one belongs makes its own demands, sets its own expectations, offers its own lures. Each pilgrim must constantly choose one goal from among many.

That choice determines the road he will take. His autobiography achieves whatever unity it may have within the context of incessant conflict, in which the opening of one door automatically closes many others. His story is made up of successive and competing stories, of successive and competing vocations. In such a succession is it possible to discover an inner relation between the present experience and the whole of experience? A Russian poet affirms that this is possible, though not without its difficulties:

> For an artist eternity is something tangibly present in every fleeting fraction of time which he would gladly stop and thus make even more tangible. What causes anguish in an artist is not longing for eternity, but a temporary loss of his feeling that every second of time is, in its fullness and density, the equal of eternity itself.[15]

"Every second of time . . . eternity." Our usual perception of things puts an infinite distance between these two magnitudes. Yet the perception of the artist can be matched by the perception of any person whose steps have been guided by the compass needle of vocation. Of course his story will include the anguish of which Mandelstam speaks, but it will also include the occasional shout of joy when the connection is grasped between some casual incident and the calling. Through the subtle force of vocation he will discover with Dietrich Bonhoeffer that "the transcendent is not infinitely remote, but close at hand."[16] Any day may confront the traveler with a crisis, but that crisis may illumine ultimate meanings better than either the deadening effects of routine or the maddening effects of anarchy.

Before proceeding further in this thought experiment let us recall the interplay of these terms: pilgrim, pack, memories and hopes, autobiography, vocation. These suggest splinters of thought whenever an individual tries by quiet reflection to link an episode in his story to the totality of his experience.

Religion as a word points essentially, I think, to that area of
human experience where in one way or another man happens
upon mystery as a summons to pilgrimage . . . where he is led
to suspect the reality of splendors that he cannot name; where
he senses meanings no less overwhelming because they can
only be hinted at in myths and rituals . . . where in great
laughter perhaps and certain silences he glimpses a destination
that he can never know fully until he reaches it.[17]

A Diaspora Community

We have invited the reader to share in a thought experiment
of which the main outline now emerges. We have been exploring focal points in the consciousness of a person whose self-
image is, or can easily become, that of a pilgrim or refugee
pressing forward into an unknown future and shaping his own
autobiography as he goes, a story in which successive episodes
are connected by a more or less clear sense of direction. There
is at least one distinct weakness in this project's initial dimensions, one which we must now try to correct. Our discussion
has proceeded as if the unit of thought should be the story of
an individual. It has thus accepted as normal the disease of
modern urban society which induces us all to use the singular
"I" instead of the plural "we." City life dissolves communal
bonds and sets every person adrift to face each exigency on his
own; nothing beyond the boundaries of his own story gives
meaning to his days and nights. Of course he still belongs to
many "we" groups, but there are so many of them that none
provides him with a "family," with a primary definition of his
identity. He works in one place and sleeps in another, and the
only time when he is sufficiently alone to think his own
thoughts is when he is commuting from the one place to the
other.[18] The extended family has been succeeded by the nuclear family; now, at least in the Occident, the nuclear family
is crumbling, not simply from the impact of divorces and ex-
tramarital affairs, nor from the professional careers of both
parents, but from the withering away of mutual activities and
mutual dependencies. We used to speak of the family, the
school, the church as primary institutions of society. No

longer. Our various autobiographies show how weak those clusters have become. Our lifestyle is that of detached atoms for whom all associations have become temporary and fragmentary. It is this detachment that makes us displaced persons, nomads for whom the ancient psalmist is still spokesman:

> *Some wandered in desert wastes*
> *finding no way to a city to dwell in;*
> *hungry and thirsty*
> *their soul fainted within them.* (*Ps. 107:4-5*)

There is some justification, then, for the modern preoccupation with the individual and his search for "a city to dwell in." Even so, our analysis can be faulted in its excessive focus on the individual. That fault must be remedied by applying what has been said about the individual to those communities which shape our several stories. It may surprise the reader to discover the degree to which the foregoing analysis of an individual pilgrim applies to communities to which he belongs. Yet this discovery will not be surprising if he belongs to a community which thinks of itself as "exiles of the Dispersion" (1 Pet. 1:1), surrounded by forces hostile to its survival. Among numerous examples we mention Israel wandering in the wilderness on its flight from Egypt, the Pilgrims migrating to the bleak shores of Massachusetts Bay, or the Chinese Communists on their Long March.

> The Chinese communist society lives within a salvific story context, just as Christian societies of the west live within a salvation narrative. Nothing makes sense apart from the story and the particular shape it takes. Not to know the story is to know nothing; to know the story is to know everything. The comprehensive story . . . of communist Chinese affairs is the account of the Long March, the Chinese version of the ancient archetypal symbol of the journey . . . of the Israelites passing from Egypt to the Promised Land.[19]

How does such a community shape and safeguard its specific identity? How does it achieve a degree of stability, preserve a coherent sense of direction, move forward in confident hope?

Whatever the shape of its current agonies, the diaspora community will interpret all these within a wider context. Prominent within that context will be the memory of events in the past which produced the current alienation, and of those expectations for the future which separate this community from all others. Consciousness of a distinct beginning and end will enable it to distinguish itself from neighbors and enemies. That beginning and that end will provide unique horizons for its own story, a story that must be kept most vivid whenever survival is most in jeopardy. It must enable each member to identify himself as a member of this community, an identification strong enough to overcome the pull toward more popular and favored groups. Exiles of the dispersion must be warned against the strategies adopted by citizens of the establishment, strategies that rely on a substitution of one story for another, one set of memories and hopes, one pair of horizoning brackets for another. For the exile community to allow its members to make that substitution insures a form of communal suicide, even when it seems to constitute the only path to survival.

The exile community is not without resources in its battle to survive. It lives by a memory that is longer, more disciplined, more discerning than the memories of any individual member. So, too, its hopes have a greater range and richness, having already survived the testing of many crises. By enabling members to relate their daily experience to the totality of community experience, this resilience and courage can be enhanced. Even so, the immediate odds seem always to be on the side of the citizens of the establishment, whose perspectives are less tenuous and whose perquisites are more tangible. The surrounding culture threatens the autobiography by which any minority group seeks to render an account of its own distinctive vocation.[20]

Because of this diaspora situation, group memory becomes especially vulnerable to the same diseases as individual memory. There will be periods of amnesia when this minority will have lost its memory of separate origins and hence of its unique identity. The longer such a period lasts the more probable the death in diaspora. However, such a death may remain hidden, inasmuch as a total amnesia of its distinctive origins may enable this community to become an established institution no longer separate from the majority culture. Even so, the danger of amnesia is real; reaction to this danger often takes the form of senility. Community memory may come to stress its own distant past until its thought becomes so unreal, so defensive, so self-centered, so neurotic that members cease to receive any genuine help from its unique inheritance as they strive to meet today's dilemmas. Memories of the distant past may be clear enough, but they may have ceased to define present-day actualities. One name for this disease is archaism, another name fundamentalism. Again, the exile community may become so infatuated with the multiple novelties of the present, so obsessed with the processes of change, so desirous of becoming up-to-date on every front, that the communal story dissolves into a stream of consciousness—a stream without banks. Group identity is lost. No shared vocation elicits group decisions and its members are scattered like dust in the wind.

The hopes of such a community are susceptible to similar ailments. An amnesiac community has lost its sense of having goals different from its peer groups in a polyglot society. Its pictures of its own destiny have become so remote and unrealizable that it has substituted the aims of the surrounding society, marching to the same drummer who sets the tempo for all other groups. A senile community, by contrast, reacts so violently against that drum that it dreams of the future in archaic images designed to serve its own desperate will to survive in its contests with competing messianisms. Its hope has become a fantasy that makes its daily disciplines even more fantastic. Or, confused by the anarchy of popular fads and fancies, the exile community reacts to successive crises by a rapid alternation of goals, blessing this program and deriding that one, hallowing various transient desires with God's ultimate promise. Pragmatism and prudence are then allowed to dictate the choice of causes with which exiles should identify themselves *pro tem.* In effect this transforms the exiles into politicians, eyes fixed on the next election. There are, alas, more hopes by which a community can die than hopes by which it can realize its distinctive calling.

Such infections are especially virulent in societies that are increasingly both pluralistic and nationalistic, where competition between group and national loyalties becomes acute. In every modern nation there live peoples that are older than the nation itself. So whenever these peoples assert their distinctiveness and advance their self-interests, the strain on national unity grows. The more ominous the threat of civil conflict, the more the nation sets out to build its own defenses by totalitarian concentration on national security. The memories of the nation must be evoked in such a way as to minimize the significance of sectarian stories. The minority's autobiography must be viewed as no more than a segment of the nation's autobiography, meriting at most a laudatory chapter in "The History of the --- Nation." Because each sect within the majority culture has contacts with its own kinfolk in other nations, the nation must keep those contacts under strict surveillance. Each of these peoples has a memory and a tradition longer than those of the conglomerate, but in celebration of the nation's past the span of national memory can be heralded as if it were in fact longer and therefore more inclusive. Cultural pluralism must be defended and even praised as proof of a nation's greatness, but the nation must take care that its security blanket is not threatened by that pluralism. Claims to unique virtue and vocation, efforts to seek the liberation of an oppressed minority—such yearnings must be kept strictly secondary to the unique status and present vocation of the nation as a whole. Should its ethnic consciousness be raised too high, any minority becomes vulnerable to surveillance by FBI and CIA. Especially in time of national crisis when an external threat to the nation forces the mobilization of sectarian resources, the

Grand Inquisitor adopts the role of Lord High Executioner, and citizens who fail to bow to the transcendent glory of the nation become, actually or potentially, internal refugees confined within a concentration camp. This syndrome is apparent in large nations that have imperial pretensions in external affairs even though in domestic affairs the dynamism of plural minorities makes more and more unlikely the achievement of genuine unity.

As powerful forces, nationalism and pluralism ricochet against each other. The use of central authority to compel national unity intensifies the tendency for each subculture to become a counterculture. This very process may yet spell the end of the modern nation-state as we have known it. One might compile a list of nations in which nationalism is still regnant and another list in which sectarian rivalries have more or less destroyed the previous unity of the nation. Which list would be longer? Undoubtedly the second. Six countries can be taken as a sample of sixty others: Northern Ireland, Lebanon, Angola, the Philippines, Spain, Cyprus. Only rarely today do the interests of internal minorities coincide with the interests of the majority. Only rarely are minorities willing to submerge their own destinies for the sake of national unity (e.g., Cyprus). Rather, each minority seeks to use the state as an instrument in the realization of its own dreams. Each sect tends to view its own saga as longer and more significant than the saga of the nation (e.g., Lebanon). Because its hope for the future is separate from that of the nation, it typically views the powers of the nation as frustrating its drive toward sectarian success (e.g., Northern Ireland). If other sects seem to be content with the order achieved within the melting pot, they become in turn the enemies of each counterculture. Thus the centrifugal forces exceed the attraction of the centripetal, and national unity is splintered in the name of sectarian loyalties (e.g., Angola). Newspapers daily report such situations. Here is a nation where pluralistic drives are relatively quiescent because the subcultures are more or less content with their share of the national glory. Here, where subcultures have become rebellious countercultures, challenging the prevailing ethos, there emerges a nation with repressions characteristic of a police state appealing to law and order as plausible justification for such repressions (e.g., South Korea). And here are nations where the countercultures reject those justifications, resist those repressions, maintain the legitimacy of their own separatist causes, and tear to shreds any semblance of national unity (e.g., Rhodesia). And in the background loom the imperial powers, each seeking to derive profit from the chaos that results. Meanwhile, each item in the day's news is calculated in computers that have been programmed according to conflicting interests, whether those of a minority, a state or some multinational corporation.

Because this conflict is indigenous to every pluralistic nation-state, communal violence seethes nearer the surface than comfortable citizens suspect. And once violence breaks loose, it cannot be contained, for the power of opposing forces is too great, each feeding on its rival. When a minority accords absolute priority to its own loyalties, the nation is provoked into employing a repression that moves toward the extreme of genocide. But when such repression impels the sect to erect barricades, the civil war moves toward the extreme of an anarchy that lasts until one minority has established its sovereignty over the others (e.g., Lebanon). Once this conflict has called into play the competing ideologies and theologies of the warring minorities, negotiations must be rejected as a possible cover-up for compromise. Thus the stories by which the nation sustains its identity are incompatible with the stories essential to the self-image of its sects. One memory excludes the others; one hope can be realized only through the defeat of the others. Distinctive traditions and prophecies become self-defeating; the greater the loyalty they inspire within the group, the more somber and tragic the immediate prospect for that group. It is not surprising that in this situation the various ethnic groups again have frequent recourse to such parabolic images as exodus and exile, revolution and liberation, dispersion and ingathering.

In its conflict with the omnicompetent but repressive state, each sect becomes more than ever aware of the importance of conserving the devotion of its individual members. The sect is as strong or as weak as the fidelity or treason of its members. On how many guerillas can it count in the final test? Conversely, a person can vindicate his membership in the sect only by willingness to sacrifice everything for its unique traditions. As each genocidal majority comes to be known by its Grand Inquisitors, each refugee community comes to be known by its Grand Martyrs, its Che Guevaras. Whether one is dealing with the Ku Klux Klan in its newest edition or with the Symbionese Liberation Army in one of its protean forms, it is the individual member through whom the character of the group's autobiography is disclosed.

We observed earlier that the coherence of any autobiography stems from the sense of vocation of the biographer. The same thing is true of the group; its autobiography is as coherent as the shared vocation of its members. Only when the several vocations of its members are bound together in the shared vocation of the group does the group's story come alive. That story evaporates whenever its members cease adopting its specific vocation as their own, their emotions aroused by its memories and hopes, its unique beginnings and endings. No longer are its members genuine heirs; no longer do the fortunes of the group form the core of their autobiographies. It may retain numerical strength but it has lost the power to fulfill the tasks for which it was created. It is at the point of a shared vocation that the interdependence of a group and its members lives or dies.

So central is this term *vocation* and so corrupted by a mélange of misinterpretations, that we must clarify the sense in which we use it in this book. Since vocation is frequently confused with profession, we need to grasp the differences. A person chooses his own profession; vocation is a response to a stimulus from outside himself. Of the two terms, profession is the more objective and tangible, vocation the more subjective and intangible. Vocation is a category of evaluation; profession, of description. Civil society can easily and rightly establish the criteria of the professions, whether law or engineering or sanitation or the military. It can legislate the standards for training, the requirements for licensing, the patterns of remuneration. It even determines, more or less, the relative ranking of the professions. But vocations are beyond such measurements and ratings. Profession defines a social image, vocation a self-image. A person without a profession is no less a person; without a vocation he is much less. It is of course true that a person's vocation may lead him to choose a specific profession. The two things may thus virtually coincide, but even when they do it is wise to distinguish them. To be a pilgrim is not a profession, but it can be a vocation.

Such contrasts become even clearer when we consider the point already made, that an individual's vocation is his share in that vocation which distinguishes his community from its neighbors. A community comes into existence to fulfill its own calling; that calling antedates the calling of each member, yet each member must share in it. All are bound together in a distinctive covenant that obligates them to a common mission within and toward the surrounding society. It is by way of this shared vocation that the community becomes an extended family for each of its members, its story becoming their own, its memories and hopes creating the effective horizons of their lives. Within these horizons different assignments are given to each member, each assignment bearing a unique cluster of responsibilities; yet that very uniqueness only serves to accentuate the unity of the one vocation. One cannot say these things of a profession; one must say them of a vocation. Whereas a profession makes a person more dependent on his own resources, a vocation increases his dependence on his community.

An even more decisive difference comes into view when we ask about origins and endings. Professional life has a well-marked starting point: the completion of training and the first earned salary. Its conclusion is equally clear: retirement and the first pension check. Not so with vocational life. Some can date the moment when they became aware of their own calling, and can anticipate the time when they will render an account of it. But this period simply covers the time of their response to a call; the call itself emerges within a wider and less tangible context. And, as we have seen, that vocation is something implicit in the life of the community as a basic reason for its existence; it is therefore as old and as permanent as the community. Each pilgrim's horizons tend to fuse with the horizons of the pilgrim community, its origins in the distant past and its goals in the hazy future. To share vocation is to share this total story.[21] I find myself even more emphatic in stressing this feature than my onetime colleague, James Gustafson:

> My strong hunch is that to be human is to have a vocation, a calling; that it is to become what we now are not; that it calls for a surpassing of what we are; that apart from a *telos*, a vision of what man can and ought to do, we will flounder and decay.[22]

To avoid needless repetition in what follows, let us adopt a few shorthand expressions. We will refer to the unique horizons, the beginning and the end, which enclose the communal story and define its shared vocation, as the *p/f component*, in which *p* stands for the *primal beginnings* and *f* for the *final goal*. We view these two realities as inseparable and interdependent, since they constitute a single set of brackets. The brackets furnish a map on which each pilgrim can chart his location, a magnetic pole with which he can align his compass.

We began this thought experiment with the observation that a person tries to make sense of things by relating each day's quota of experiences to the totality of things. Often, of course, a traveler is too absorbed in immediate choices to reflect on their link to the ultimate. "Visibility: fifty feet." At times, however, that absorption evaporates and the foreground is seen in the context of a more remote background. "Visibility: ninety miles." By his memories and hopes the wanderer becomes aware of earlier and later episodes in a continuous story. Yet if he limits the totality of things to the time of his own life, these limits are altogether too restrictive to provide the required range. That range approaches adequacy only when the *communal* p/f component provides the genuine horizons for each individual traveler. Those horizons are broader than his own birth and death; they may be broader than the birth and demise of a nation, or even than the Toynbeean measurements of the rise and fall of a civilization. By sharing the communal vocation, each member shares the story of a whole world of reality.

Since the p/f component expresses both horizons, fore and aft, we will at times need another shorthand expression to distinguish the separate horizons, the fore from the aft, the p from the f. For this purpose we will use an alphabetical symbol, drawing on a practice that is very old indeed. The p or primal factor will be symbolized by the first three letters in the English alphabet and the f or final factor by the last three letters (ABC, XYZ). By using three letters in each case we will be able to distinguish three separate features in the memories of origins, and three features in anticipations of the end. To cover the intervening period, the intervening span of the community's story, we will use the symbol CMX. With the help of these symbols we turn now to a hypothetical map of a group's autobiography.

The P/F Component

If the lifetime of the exile community is visualized in horizontal terms, it can be reduced to a simple diagram:

$$P \qquad\qquad\qquad F$$
$$ABC \leftarrow CMX \rightarrow XYZ$$

In this diagram CMX is intended to cover almost the whole span of a particular community's story, both communal and individual. Within this span we may assign all the various tasks, dilemmas and obstacles encountered in the course of fulfilling its vocation. Though oriented toward its p/f component, this vocation is always to be conjugated in the present tense, the immediate routines and pressures, the continuing period of trials and turmoil, which fidelity to vocation engenders. Yet the maintenance of present fidelity requires an open and constant access to the power that flows from the p/f horizons.

It is possible for a community to identify these horizons with the beginning and the ending of all things. To give this ultimate context to its vocation, however, is to become fully and explicitly religious, to make a religious commitment and to orient all existence around that assertion. There have been communities for whom a basic image of God has been conveyed by the Aleph and Tau of the Hebrew alphabet or the Alpha and Omega of the Greek. These communities have recognized that their god stands as Creator not alone at their own distinctive beginning but at all origins, and as Redeemer not alone at their own end but at the end of all things. God is that *One* before whom all generations rise and pass away; of his kingdom there is neither an end nor a beginning. A consequence of this seemingly audacious claim is belief in the universal and cosmic significance of the communal vocation, which then, by implication, confers an ultimate significance to the story of each member. From this vision of the p/f component all experiences during the CMX zone derive an imponderable weight, whether negative or positive. This is to say that the will of the God who stands at the A and the Z becomes a normative standard to be applied to each thought and deed during the CMX. This constant link between each event and its ultimate context may be illustrated by a simple table grace which may be quite casually muttered before the hurried meal of a preoccupied and distraught family, but which yet recognizes each slice of bread as the gift of the Most High God sharing heavenly manna with his people.

In our thought experiment we now move, therefore, from the analysis of all communities to the analysis of explicitly religious communities which are grounded in a monotheistic faith. In due time we will move from a hypothetical religion to a specific religion. But first we should carry a step further the hypothetical appraisal, asking what problems of thought such

a community faces whenever it claims that the story of its own
life and vocation embodies God's calling and promise for the
whole created world. Four problematic areas appear to be
inescapable.

1. When a community identifies its own p/f component with
that of the whole creation, we must ask how that community
gains a convincing access to that component sufficient to em-
power and validate its own vocation. No human community is
in itself eternal. Though its longevity may exceed that of individual members, though it may exceed even that of a nation-
state, it bears within itself the seeds of decay and mortality. Its
thoughts are permeated and perverted by its own transiency.
This being so, how can it perceive any absolute beginning or
ending? Any such perception must be gained during the present period when it is subjected to the corrosive effects of
tumult and tragedy. Historical relativism is a factor to be reck-
oned with, whether or not one is a disciple of Freud or Nietz-
sche or Marx. All ideas are subject to influence from social
phobias and neuroses, so that each effort to describe the ABC
of all creation is an invitation to scepticism if not derision; it
sounds like the "once upon a time" of a bedtime story. So, too,
each version of the XYZ sounds like "they lived happily ever
after." Since all human experience lies within the CMX, we
wonder whether any version of the p/f component can be
trusted. The more turbulent the present, the more urgent that
question becomes—and the more dubious the answers. We
must reckon with the collision between these two convictions:
on the one hand it is quite impossible to comprehend the
whole story without perceiving its p/f horizons; on the other
hand it is quite impossible for actors within the story to experience those horizons. Can any community, however old or wise,
solve that riddle? It would seem that it can be solved, if at all,
only through unusually keen perceptions on the part of some
select individuals. We will call this first problem, then, the
problem of revelatory agents,[23] prophets entitled to disclose
what no eye has seen and no ear heard.

2. Let us assume the emergence of such agents and assume

also that they have discerned the character of the p/f component. Now a problem appears as to how they will be able to communicate this discovery to the other members of the community, persons whose ability to comprehend is limited to their own vantage point within the CMX zone. When prophets glimpse what no other eye has seen, how will they communicate that vision to those other eyes? When they hear something others have not heard and when they try to share it, will others be deaf to it? Does the transcendent inevitably lose its transcendence when drawn within the ordinary range of the immanent? Or, if it preserves its strangeness, will it forever remain unintelligible? Again it is obvious that the more turbulent the CMX situation into which knowledge of the p/f component is inserted, the more acute the hazards. We may glibly chant "As it was in the beginning, is now, and ever shall be," but such a chant advertises a most audacious claim. What is meant by that language? Either it seems too vague to have much bearing on present bewilderments or it seems so specific that it invites ridicule and rejection. Language must be used, to be sure; but since all language has been developed within the confines of a human story, no terminology is readily available for describing realities outside those confines. We are seldom aware of the complexities of this problem because we seldom visualize ourselves as revelatory agents and we seldom encounter such "see-ers," except perhaps as easily recognized crackpots who announce world's end tomorrow. Yet the problem remains: how to choose revelatory language that can disclose the p/f component in such a way as to convey accurate knowledge of the essential brackets of the communal story and vocation.

3. Reflection on these first two problems would seem to dictate another conclusion: perception of the story's beginning-and-end and communication of that perception as a guide to vocation become possible only when something happens *within* the brackets of human experience that discloses the p/f horizons. It is not by gazing into stratospheric space or by a fancied flight into timeless regions that a community

discerns the transcendent. To be valid, any perception of ABC and XYZ must be grasped within CMX. But of course that raises difficult questions of where and how. *Where* do we see the eternal superimposed on the temporal? *How* can the p/f perspective on *all* things be disclosed within the small compass of a *single* thing? Or is it not a form of madness to find within a single story the pattern of all stories? The claim that some event has power to clarify all events would seem to be the only alternative to an incredible feat in space-science fiction. Yet to advance such a claim always seems to be an effort to exploit the community's egoistic cravings and credulities. So here again we face a major collision. Only within some event (some "dogpatch outside a city wall" [Auden]) within CMX can the p/f component be discerned; yet all such events seem too small to fulfill so grandiose a function. Here the problem is that of locating a *revelatory event* within the CMX zone which can clarify the p/f component, a disclosure situation to which we may now assign another shorthand term: M-event.

4. Yet another problem presents itself. Let us assume that the M-event has been discovered, that it is perceptible and communicable to the community as a whole and that it serves to clarify the p/f component. Not only must this event be uniquely capable of disclosing primal and final realities; it must also be fully able to illuminate in some degree all occasions. It must be sufficiently paradigmatic to represent all experiences of all men; this means that those experiences must somehow be present within it.

> *With nature as with man, to know*
> *One moment's aspect is to show*
> *All of nature, all of man,*
> *A wheel that turns again, again.*
> *The smallest speck turned inside out*
> *Can spin the universe about,*
> *And myriad atoms, one by one,*
> *Copy the planets and the sun.* [24]

Or considering the special story and the special vocation of a given community, the paradigmatic event must suggest a pattern basic to its inner and outer occasions. More than this, it is not truly paradigmatic for the community unless it demonstrates a continuing power to penetrate and illumine the several stories of each member of that community. One event must be capable of providing a cohesive and pervasive theme for every autobiography; it must disclose the miraculous fusion of daily experience and the totality of experience, both communal and existential. It is far from easy to think of any single event that could have such capacity. The hazards seem too great for us to accept any transient event as revealing the teleology implicit in all cosmic, communal, and personal stories. The problem is an obvious one: the *paradigmatic adequacy of the M-event.*

It should be clear that none of these difficulties can be met apart from the use of an active and disciplined imagination, which transcribes what happens to people into story-form, and which is then able to sense correlations that are hidden within and behind many separate stories. The life of each sojourning person or community comprises a small story.[25] If that larger story should point backward to the creation of all things and forward to an inclusive end, if it should provide an event at the mid-point where the figural imagination discerns an intersection with all smaller stories, then sojourners should be able to locate themselves on this larger narrative map. But perhaps our imaginations are too drugged by modern barbiturates for such activity.[26]

By viewing these problems together—the necessity for revelatory agents, for clarifying language, for an M-event having paradigmatic adequacy—we get a more profound sense of the massive difficulties in gaining a dependable sense of the origin and end of all things. Yet the more the contemporary maze frustrates those necessities, the more essential becomes some vision of the beginnings of the various stories.

If theologians are correct,
A Plan implies an Architect:
A God-built maze would be, I'm sure
The Universe in miniature. [27]

Mr. Auden suggests that when we are caught within such a maze, that very predicament seems to presuppose a time before the maze was built, along with its building and the confusions following that construction. In present conflicts a prior peace appears to be implicit, followed by some disruption of that peace. It becomes necessary to suppose that there was a time *before* time went askew, a time *when* time went askew, and a time *since.* All of these times antedate my time, our time and the time of our world—in fact, the whole of the CMX zone. The question concerning the p factor, the character of the ABC reality, appears thus to comprise at least three distinguishable features:

The A: What was the original situation before any disruption, what was the character of creation before any rebellion?

The B: What forces first sparked the rebellion and constituted the skewing of time?

The C: How did that disruption alter the human situation, producing the maze within which humanity now lives?

All questions concerning the beginnings appear to involve some set of ideas that will embrace these three features. It becomes difficult for the human mind to remain human without exploring those features.

Difficult, yes. Yet most of us do in fact avoid such explorations and we rationalize our avoidance by assuming in advance the futility of the search. All such questions strike us as being too abstruse, too speculative. We don't have time for such woolgathering. We are not unlike a four-year-old child in dialogue with his mother:

Mother: Son, *that* happened before you were born.

Child: Before I was this long? (Hands extended thirty inches apart.)

Mother: No, much earlier than that.

Child: Before I was this long? (Hands extended fifteen inches apart.)

Mother: No, before you were here at all. There wasn't any you.

Child: Mom, quit teasing me!

Not only are we unable to remember our own birth; we are even less able to imagine existence itself before our birth.

This is perhaps why Buddhists are invited to meditate on a particular koan: "Where were you before your father met your mother?" Such a question permits no simple answer and perhaps no answer at all. We don't readily tolerate questions like that. And there may be canny wisdom in such intolerance.

> *What kingdom can be reached by the occasions*
> *That climb the broken ladders of our lives?*
> *We are imprisoned in unbounded spaces,*
> *Defined by an indefinite confusion.* [28]

Yet how can our story have coherence unless it has a definite starting point? Whence comes vocation if not from some hidden source? A knot must be made in the thread before we can begin to sew (Kierkegaard). To be content with total ignorance concerning our own beginnings can be very costly, if not fatal.

The obstacles to discerning an ABC are matched by the problem of discerning an XYZ. If our location within the maze prevents looking over the hedges into areas outside the maze, the same location prevents a vision of the situation after we have left the maze. The restoration of peace after the rebellion must in some definite way correspond to the original fracturing of the peace. Logic dictates that eschatological realities should correspond to the protological, uniting the ABC and the XYZ in a single perspectival whole. The dynamics of the story demand it, and so do the realities of vocation. The design of the new age must be consonant with the original design of creation, that is, if the creative forces are ever to overcome the rebellious forces. So in a hypothetical way we may distinguish certain features in our alphabetical symbol of the end:

The X: In what event(s) may be discerned evidence that the conflict is being terminated, that a decisive change has happened or is imminent?

The Y: What forces are capable of responding to this change in such a way as to extend the victory over the rebellious forces?

The Z: What will be the character and design of the new creation following the cessation of hostilities? On what terms may the resources of that creation be appropriated now?

It is difficult even to pose these questions, as it is difficult for minds inured to conflict to comprehend a world at peace, and difficult to imagine programs by which that peace might be assured. An absolute future is as remote from present involvements as an absolute past. Finite and temporal immediacies distort any reflections on the infinite and eternal.

These distortions are well depicted by Russell Baker in one of his columns in the *New York Times*.[29] He pictures a typical American family reacting to the news of the end of the world, as it gathers around the TV at a rather unusual hour.

> It is 1 o'clock in the morning. For months the networks have tried to persuade the world to end in prime time. "In prime time," they said, "it could top the ratings of the Super Bowl." No dice. The end of the world is not like the Republican National Convention. It is the last thing left that can say no to television.

Baker has caught the ironies involved whenever we try to speak of a final event. It is surely an instance of prime time, but it conflicts with all human conceptions of what makes a time prime. The final event can be visualized only as an event in the sequence of known events, but to do that is to destroy its genuine finality.

> President Ford will address the nation in a few minutes. According to NBC . . . he will say that the end of the world is an historic event for all Americans. The children are restless. They would rather watch "Abbott and Costello Meet Frankenstein" on Channel 8. Foolish, foolish childhood.

To call the end of the world "historic" is to trivialize it, and to narrow its scope. To say "for all Americans" is to betray the inevitable parochialism of thought about ultimate matters. A presidential address on such an occasion betrays foolishness greater even than that of the children.

> John Chancellor is showing film clips of the events leading to the night's event. Pictures of the last oil well going dry. Of the earth's vitally essential ozone layer breaking down under aerosol gases. Of well-dressed men carrying briefcases paying $5 admission to pornographic movies.

What an infinite distance between these trivia and the actualities of world's end. Is it possible to conceive of the end as belonging to the same sequence as such other events? If so, it becomes available to film clips, comparable to using an aerosol can. If not, where and how does it gear into the casual movements of men and women?

> "Just think," says mother, "when we all get up tomorrow morning, the world will have ended." "Just like yesterday morning," says grandmother.

Which of those two remarks conveys more sense? Actually, both show how incomprehensible is speech about eschatological reality, so long as one retains the usual sequence of days as the baseline of thought, as constituting the unchanging rhythm of reality.[30]

> Mother wants to switch to CBS. She feels that so long as Walter Cronkite is handling the end of the world, everything will turn out all right.

Thus is reflected the public's acceptance of TV commentators as people qualified to serve as apostles and prophets, since they can be trusted with special knowledge and power to keep the future under control.

Baker's wisdom and wit make it very clear that if we were to ignore the hypothetical requirements which we have analyzed, our thinking about the p/f component would make no sense at all. That is to say, there must first be some clarification of the problems. There must be a revelatory *agent*, using revelatory *language* to interpret an *M-event* in such a way as to disclose its *paradigmatic relevance* for the vocation of a community and its individual members. A modern poet has well expressed the difficulties in the following terms, terms which summarize the discussion in this chapter.

> *The Pilgrim Way has led to the Abyss.*
> *We who must die demand a miracle.*
> *How could the Eternal do a temporal act,*
> *The Infinite become a finite fact?*
> *Nothing can save us that is possible:*
> *We who must die demand a miracle.* [31]

There is no point in underestimating the complexities of those requirements, but there is also no point in underestimating the cost of settling for something less than their solution. When people are denied all knowledge of an ultimate whence and whither, it becomes impossible for them to get their bearings. If no contact exists with a reality transcending their anarchies and apathies, they are consigned to permanent slavery to them. To deny a beginning and an end to our warring is to assign eternal status to fratricidal conflict; we become like dayflies and lightning bugs.

The testimony of the Bible summons us to recognize that all the problems we have mentioned are soluble only in terms of a faith in a god. Without such a god we are hopeless in the world, as the apostle testifies (Eph. 2:12).

All talk about ultimate things, the p/f component, is actually god-talk. And unless one's talk bears on the character of that component it is not god-talk at all, however ponderous and theological it may sound. And such god-talk quickly ceases to be theoretical and hypothetical. So we must now leave the contours of a hypothetical thought experiment in order to consider the more tangible testimonies of specific revelatory agents who have used revelatory language to describe what was to them the M-event. We turn, then, to the New Testament prophets seeking to comprehend their versions of the story within which the Christian community was "called to the one hope that belongs to your calling" (Eph. 4:4).

PART II
The New Creation

Totality of meaning and cosmic drama are the two keys that will help us unlock the myths of the Beginning and the End. [1]

To handle theological metaphor aright is to be both traditional and experimental. [2]

2
The Clarifying Event
Acts 3:15

*The understanding of the crucified Jesus
must be the origin of all Christology,
for otherwise his death on the cross
would mean the end of all Christology.* [1]

Here we move from patterned logic to an actual story, from a
hypothetical analysis of ideas to a description of the thought
of specific thinkers. Having chosen five central texts, one for
each of the following chapters, we will see how those texts
epitomize the thought of those writers. In this present chapter
we focus upon one verse from Peter's address, testing first its
relation to the entire address and then its linkage to the
thought of the entire New Testament. The verse is this:

> You killed the Author of life, whom God raised from the dead.
> To this we are witnesses. *(Acts 3:15)*

Here three acts are distinguished from each other and yet
are linked together: an act of murder, an act of resurrection,
an act of testimony. Each act is an episode in a separate story, each story having a distinct subject: you . . . God . . . we.
Yet those separate stories have a point of contact; they all
deal with a single person who is identified by an unusual
phrase as the Author of life. Because of this point of
contact the three clauses form a highly condensed epit-

ome of a single story which we must examine carefully.

The first readers would have understood without difficulty who these three subjects were, but modern readers may need a bit of help. So first a word about these subjects. *"You* killed. . . ." Peter hurls against his audience a charge of murder which is meant to be taken with total seriousness. Against whom is the charge leveled? Like the other writers of the New Testament, Luke rarely writes for a general audience; he normally singles out a specific group so that the words can become an episode in the story of that group.[2] That is surely the case here. The audience is the "men of Israel" in whose presence a cripple has been healed. They are worshipers gathered in the temple at the hour of prayer—praying murderers. Yet Peter addresses them also as his own brothers, brothers for whom God has raised up a prophet. To be sure, they had turned that prophet over to the hated Romans, had said no when Pilate desired to release him, had instead asked amnesty for a murderer, and had killed Jesus. Even so, Peter continues to view these murderers as sons of the prophets and heirs of the covenant. Because they stand in mortal danger of being destroyed "from the people," he calls them to repentance. The pivot of thought is perfectly clear: the story of the covenant people has reached a climax at the point where this speaker issues the charge of murder and the call to repentance.

We should note that Peter did not stop to prove that each individual auditor had been present in Pilate's court, demanding death for Jesus. Rather, he seemed to have assumed their guilt as men of Israel and brothers. In fact, Peter probably included in this wider audience Israelites who were not even present in Jerusalem on that day; he addressed all Israel from the time of the fathers (v. 13) to the coming times of refreshing (v. 19). *"You* killed. . . ." The pronoun covers the entire story of Israel. But Peter is not primarily interested in condemning them, for he makes it clear that it is to them first that God had sent his risen Son. It is to save them that God has sent his servant to Israel. So Peter defines this *you* both by the people's act of murder and by God's act of mercy.

"Whom *God* raised. . . ." It is clear that to Peter, as to earlier prophets, the saga of Israel had become fused with the story of God. As Israel was not mankind in general, but a particular people, so this God was no deity in general, but the One who had revealed to them his very name. He is the God of their fathers, of Abraham, Isaac, and Jacob (v. 13). He had bound himself to them by specific actions which formed the horizons of their existence as his people. His vocation provided the time and space boundaries of this people. From his initial call he had kept firmly in mind his promise to bless both Abraham's posterity and all the families of the earth (v. 25). The speech assumes that nothing could be more determinative of Israel's destiny than the overarching purposes of this Ruler who was as immediately present to these auditors at that moment as he had been to Moses or to Abraham. His transcendence does not remove him from this temple scene, but rather links this "where" to his "everywhere." His action guarantees that this moment in Israel's experience is linked to the totality of Israel's history.

In this respect Peter assumes the same attitude toward God's distance-and-nearness as Isaiah had:

> *The Lord is the everlasting God,*
> *the Creator of the ends of the earth.*
>   . . . .
> *He gives power to the faint*
> *and to him who has no might he increases strength.*
> *(Isa. 40:28–29)*

Or, in the idiom of Psalm 90, since God has been Israel's dwelling place in all generations, today's trouble and joy bind Israel to the time "before the mountains were brought forth" (vv. 2, 14). It is because of his longevity that God can teach them to "number their days," can disclose his work to them, can establish the work of their hands. This people can "get a heart of wisdom" by recognizing the vocation to which he calls them.

"*We* are witnesses. . . ." Who speaks here? Not Christians accusing Jews in self-righteous indignation. Rather, Jews who had met the risen Lord, speaking to Jews who had not. They were separated not by merit but by a vision, and the result was a difference in attitudes toward Jesus' death. Peter's audience obviously interpreted that death in a way different from Peter. To them it was no murder at all, but an act in line with their loyalty to Abraham, to Moses, and especially to the God of Israel. They saw Jesus not as "the Author of life" but as a false prophet, a pretender, a deceiver, an insidious threat to both Israel and the God of Israel. They probably thought they were obeying specific commands of Scripture with regard to the treatment of false prophets (e.g., Deut. 13:1–5). In short, their sense of vocation presumably was as strong as Peter's.

At issue was Jesus' death. The significance of that death depended upon what Jesus' vocation had been prior to that death. And that, in turn, depended upon the will of the hidden God. For Peter and John the issue had been settled once for all by God's act in glorifying his servant and in sending him back to the very Israel that had murdered him. From the beginning of his work Jesus had been God's servant, the Holy and Righteous One, the Author of life. The resurrection was God's way of clarifying that identity, and his way of calling Peter and John to report this clarification to their brothers. The conflict between Peter and his audience could therefore be expressed in these terms: "You acted in terms of your vocation; we are acting in terms of ours." Because of the strength of these incompatible vocations a sharp conflict was inevitable.

Even so, while Peter and his audience had not shared the encounter with the risen Lord, they did in fact share much common ground. Peter could count on some common memories of Jesus' work before Golgotha. He could also appeal to the cure of the cripple, the actuality of which did not seem to be contested by his opponents (Acts 3:1–10). He recognized a common loyalty to Scripture, to the covenant with Abraham, and to all the prophets since Samuel. All Israel recognized the central role of these prophets as the eyes and head of Israel

(Isa. 29:10). Step by step in Israel's pilgrimage these prophets had made audible the inaudible guidance of God, mediating to the people such a knowledge of beginnings and endings as would control their memories and hopes. It was their common loyalty to a hidden God that made reliance upon the prophets so important, for apart from prophetic vision God's purposes could not be discerned: His path is on the waters, but his footsteps are unseen (Ps. 77:19).

It was wholly logical, then, for Peter to appeal to authorities which his audience also respected: "what God foretold by the mouth of all the prophets." All agreed on the validity of the prophets' promises. Yet this agreement accentuated the confrontation between speaker and audience.

> What God foretold by the mouth of all the prophets, *that his Christ should suffer, he thus fulfilled. (v. 18)*

Peter was bound to say this; they were bound to reject it. The matter at issue was the suffering of Jesus.

Perhaps Peter's reference to "all the prophets" was too general and too vague. When he appealed to one of the promises issued by one of the prophets, he became more definite and concrete.

> Moses said, "The Lord God will raise up for you a prophet from your brethren as he raised me up. *(v. 22; cf. Deut. 18:15, 18)*

Together with Peter, his auditors had accepted Moses' promise; but they had not found it fulfilled in the resurrection of Jesus. For them no successor to Moses had appeared (Deut. 34:10); for Peter he had come.

Here speaker and listeners collided head-on. But we should not allow this fact to cover up the agreement that prevailed on several other points. Peter and his listeners agreed in regarding Moses as the fountainhead of prophecy, the supreme *revelatory agent* of God. Among the promises of God, the promise issued to Moses at Sinai and in the wilderness wanderings was one on which they especially relied. The identification of the exodus from Egypt as the pivotal *revelatory event* was another item of agreement. Throughout the entire span of Israel's history (the CMX era, to use our shorthand), this liberation had served as the pivotal M-event. Israel could conceive of only one answer to the series of rhetorical questions in Deuteronomy 4:32–40: "Has such a great thing as this ever happened or been heard of? Did any people ever hear the voice of a god speaking out of the midst of the fire?" It had been this event that had clarified the vocation of this people and the power of this God, and had provided both a map and rations for their long journey. Israel accepted that vocation anew on every Sabbath and at every annual festival.

The agreement between Peter and his audience extended to the use of a distinctive *revelatory language,* an archetypal saga in which the storytellers recounted the signs and wonders by which God had broken Pharaoh's bitter yoke, had opened a path through the Red Sea, had provided the pillars of fire and cloud for the wilderness safari, and had given them a home in the land of milk and honey. If Israel had forgotten this prophet, this event, this saga or the vocation intrinsic to it, it would have vanished utterly. At the end of the saga both Peter and his hearers anticipated an entrance into "times of refreshing from the presence of the Lord" (3:19).

Nor did they disagree on the adequacy of this M-event to provide paradigmatic guidance for the nation. To be sure, major altercations took place among various groups within Israel: Sadducees, Pharisees, Zealots, Essenes, and doubtless other groups. But for all of them God's gift of liberation through Moses retained its power to define both ultimate horizons and immediate duties. Moses remained for the communal conscience a bond of unity and an arbiter of a vocation that marked off this people from all others.

What was true for the nation was true for each Israelite. In observing the Passover each celebrated his own deliverance from captivity, together with the hope for his own homecoming. Each observance of the Sabbath was an act of identification with the Twelve Tribes and an acceptance of the authority of Moses. Whenever he heard the Scripture read in the synagogue, he could align his own pilgrimage afresh to the calling of the ancestral community.

> Not with our fathers did the Lord make this covenant, but with us, who are all of us here alive this day. *(Deut. 5:3)*

Did the conversational partners agree on the relevance of the M-event to the universal story of God's dealings with mankind? Did the Exodus saga point to a divinely determined design for all human communities? Here the answer must be negative, at least in part. It is never easy for any people to transcend its own conflicts of interest. Many of Peter's listeners probably felt that God's promises to Israel excluded the Gentiles and that any form of universalism would destroy the unique calling of Israel. Certainly there were many Jewish Christians who believed that the revelation through Moses had been limited to Jews. Luke's portrait of Peter in Acts 10 indicates that even he required further clarification of this point. On the other hand, it is likely that there were non-Christian Jews who believed that the liberation of Israel in God's plan would ultimately include the liberation of all nations. This point of view is implicit in the Deuteronomic vision which stresses the conviction that there is no other god in heaven or on earth but "our God" and that he is the Lord of all nations (Deut. 4:32–40). This conviction becomes even clearer in later prophetic interpretations of the M-event (cf. Isa. 40–55).

However that may be, it is clear that the common ground between Peter and his audience was very extensive. It is also clear that this common ground made the points at issue all the more controversial; and especially the witness to the resurrection, which carried with it the clarification of what had happened in the death of Jesus. Peter knew, of course, that his appeal to the miraculous cure would be insufficient to carry conviction, as would be his appeal to all the prophets and even his explicit citation of Moses' promise. Luke had made it clear that the apostles themselves had not understood the necessity "that this Christ should suffer," at least not until after the Risen Lord had so instructed them (Lk. 24:25, 26, 44–49). At that exact time the Messiah had commissioned them to witness to God's glorification of the "prophet like Moses" whom Israel had rejected. Everything now hinged on the reliability of their witness. In other words, Peter had been commissioned as a revelatory agent to interpret a revelatory event in such revelatory language that he would clarify for this audience the paradigmatic adequacy of that event for defining their vocation.[3]

The Resurrection of the Crucified

The centrality of this event should be obvious. *If* God has thus glorified his servant Jesus, he has made the sufferings of Jesus the clue for understanding all his earlier covenants and promises. *If* God has raised this prophet from the dead, then God has given his verdict concerning the guilt of the assassins. *If* this crucified person has become Lord, he has been sent to this people as the prophet like Moses, with final authority for them. A vision of the Risen Jesus would in effect be a command for those who have seen him to testify to those who have not. For these witnesses, this event would tend to displace the Exodus as the clarifying center (M-event) of the story; or it would be better to say that the event of Exodus would now be reinterpreted in the light of this humiliation-exaltation. As the prophet clarified one event he would be clarifying the other as well. Moreover, in this clarification the newly ordained prophet would deal with the two events (you killed . . . God raised) either as twin events or as one interlocking event. Certainly there would be a single story, in which neither the murder nor the vindication nor the witness could be understood in isolation. An unbelieving audience would inevitably separate Jesus' death from his glorification, since they would accept the actuality of the one but not of the other. But the vocation of believers would begin only when they accepted the union of the two. They were called to announce the resurrection as God's gracious offer to redeem the very people who had murdered his son.

The various descriptions of this event, along with its various implications as set forth in the New Testament, will be the object of exploration throughout the remainder of this chapter. To enter into such an exploration requires that we become extremely flexible in vocabulary and versatile in linguistic idiom. Although modern practice tends to concentrate on one term, *resurrection,* this is far from being the only metaphor used in Scripture. I have spoken of metaphor with malice aforethought. It may create resistance on the part of readers for whom metaphorical language is inherently less impressive than literal language. But in dealing with such an event as this, I must agree with my friend Roger Hazelton that "no possibility of substituting literal for metaphorical language exists." The term *resurrection* is "a metaphor gone slack from millennia of overuse," like the metaphor "the face of the earth." When we use terms like these, it is probably true that "our thinking is most metaphorical when we are least aware that it is so."[4]

Any mystery as profound as resurrection calls into play the use of numerous metaphors. Speech that is limited to one of these soon becomes poverty-stricken. Fortunately, in this case there is a wide range of alternatives. New Testament witnesses often spoke of God exalting Jesus, or anointing or glorifying or sanctifying him. Each of these verbs (and verbs are usually more apt than nouns) had a different range of figural associations, although none of them became a standard or requisite term. Writers often compared what had happened to an awakening or an arousing from sleep, or to a translation or ascension to heaven. They spoke of it as a manifestation or a disclosure of God's presence, his power, his wisdom, his election. Or they said that Jesus had been enthroned, had put on immortality, had been assumed into heaven, had gone to the Father. He had been given a name above all other names. Many nouns expressed different nuances in his victory: he has become ruler, judge, author of life, head over all things, the second Adam, the first-born from the dead. The proliferation of images used to refer to this event is a measure of its mysterious depths. Whenever we limit our vocabulary to one of those

metaphors we betray our own superficiality and provinciality.
To catch the first witnesses in the act of thinking about this
event we need to be as imaginative as they were in drawing
upon multiple analogies, and as discriminating as they in plac-
ing each analogy within its own native habitat. The event was
so paradigmatic that all thinking became magnetized by it; yet
it was also so unprecedented as to make each separate metaphor quite inadequate.

Our imagination will profit from noticing the biblical tendency, in referring to this event, to use antitheses, paired metaphors whose positive and negative nuances complement each
other. Already in Acts 3:15 we have noted one such pair: you
killed . . . he raised. Man's act had been negated by God's;
God's act had disclosed the real character of man's. When we
observe the variety of these twin analogies, our thinking may
be freed from customary shibboleths. Here is a partial list:

death	life	first Adam	second Adam
shame	glory	putting off the old	putting on the new
humiliation	exaltation	physical body	spiritual body
weakness	power	the perishable	the imperishable
sleep	awakening	destruction	restoration
descent	ascent	rejection	election
defeat	victory	exile	homecoming
suffering	glory	baptized into death	raised into life
bondage	freedom	put to death in flesh	made alive in spirit
captivity	captors captured	to go away	to come again
corruption	incorruption	mortality	immortality
man of dust	man of heaven		

Although one might expand or reduce this list or challenge some of its entries, the values of such a list should be recognized. Each antithesis reminds us that we cannot comprehend what had happened without recalling Jesus' story as a whole. Also, the conviction is reinforced that this is a twin event, in which death and resurrection are inseparable and interdependent. The conjunction of opposites makes of each pair a single compound metaphor. To take each compound metaphor seriously requires a change in thinking about both segments: references to "this" death are as *metaphorical* in character as references to "this" resurrection, and, conversely, references to "this" resurrection are as *realistic* as references to "this" death. At least this is so when we try to cope with the conviction that God was the hidden actor in both events. The list also illustrates how quite ordinary words were used to describe quite extraordinary matters. In one sense the linguistic features of the testimony are entirely usual, in another sense most unusual. Finally, the list of antonyms suggests the paradigmatic complexity of the event. In its New Testament context each compound metaphor has a direct bearing upon the experience of each believer, as well as upon the experience of the community as a whole (e.g., the terms *weakness-power*). Furthermore, because the ultimate actor in the event is asserted to be God, each compound metaphor has at least an indirect bearing upon the experience of creation as a whole, all "tribes and tongues and peoples and nations." We hope to make some of these connections transparent in later chapters of this book.[5]

Of course, these twin metaphors appear in specific literary contexts, each context indicating a sequence of events within which this event belonged. In any story the significance of an event derives in part from its place in the total sequence of events. Let us now, therefore, scan the sequence in the story as recounted by five different writers.

In Acts 3 the story moves through several stages: the God of our fathers . . . the Author of life . . . the covenant with Abraham . . . the promise to Moses and to other prophets

. . . the sending of Jesus . . . his rejection by Israel . . . his glorification . . . the appointment of witnesses . . . the cure of the cripple . . . the demand for repentance . . . the sending of Christ . . . the times of refreshing. As we noted above, Peter places the event of resurrection at the center of several stories: of God, of Israel, of the vocation of the witnesses, of the paralyzed man, of the murderers themselves. This one event has the power to unify many stories which otherwise would be entirely separate.

The author of Hebrews 11 and 12 utilized a different idiom in writing to a different audience, in this case some dilatory and despondent followers of Jesus: the creation of the world by the word of God . . . the appearance of the visible out of the invisible . . . the faith of pilgrims, beginning with Abel . . . the gift of children to Abraham and Sarah . . . the faith of Moses . . . the escape from Egypt and the capture of Jericho . . . the continued delay of the promise . . . the joy set before Jesus . . . his endurance of the cross . . . his enthronement at God's right hand . . . our struggle with sin . . . the running of the race . . . God's discipline of his sons . . . the perfecting of faith . . . the share in Jesus' holiness, blessing and kingdom. Again we note a single inclusive story having a distinctive beginning and end. The unifying element in that story is God's call, followed by Israel's response; the clarifying element is Jesus' endurance and enthronement.

Very different is the scenario in John 14, where in a portion of Jesus' farewell to his disciples he indicates the wider context for his departure: "I am the way, the truth, the life . . . no one comes to the Father but by me . . . I go to prepare a place for you . . . the ruler of this world is coming . . . he has no power over me . . . I do as the Father has commanded . . . the world will see me no more, but you will see me . . . I will pray to the Father . . . He will give you another Counselor . . . I go to the Father . . . because I live, you will live also . . . you will do greater works than these . . . I will come again . . . I will take you to myself." From this sequence it is impossible to recover a single chronological order; the changes that are recorded are changes in the relation of Jesus to his Father, to his followers, to the ruler of this world. Yet those changes have a sequence of their own. Jesus comes and goes and comes; by this movement he becomes the Way for them. Life is defined not by the calendar but by his presence with his own, and by his taking them to himself. The bond created by his word and by their love links each moment in their stories to the eternal purposes of the Father.[6]

The First Epistle of Peter is written to exiles of the dispersion who are facing the fires of social hostility, legal persecution, and violent death. It relates their vocation of suffering to that of Jesus. Looking only at the first chapter, we may note this sequence: God's will . . . his calling of Christ before creation . . . his election of the faithful . . . the prophets' prediction of Christ's sufferings . . . the manifestation of Christ at the end of time . . . the ransom by his blood . . . his resurrection . . . the descent of the Spirit . . . the preaching of the gospel . . . the new birth of believers . . . their trials, sufferings, obedience, love, joy . . . the salvation coming at the revelation of Christ. The p/f component is made very clear; the character of the M-event is equally clear. The stories of the exiles in various remote provinces receive their essential meaning from the story of God's election and from the acts of grace by which he fulfills his promises through suffering.

An equally broad panorama comes into view in Colossians 1. Christ's presence with God at the beginning is affirmed in various ways. He is the image of the invisible God, the first-born of all creation, the one through whom all things were created and in whom all things hold together. His work for men is described in terms of his being the first-born from the dead, the one through whom God is reconciling all things to himself. In him dwells all the fullness of God; he is the head of all things and of his body, the church. The author sees his own sufferings as direct participation in the sufferings of Christ, through whose death the readers have been reconciled. Their vocation is in turn defined by their "Head": he calls them to continue in the faith, to lead a life worthy of the Lord, to make known the glorious mystery among the Gentiles. At the end they will be presented before God "holy and blameless" through the benefits of Christ's sufferings if only they remain faithful to the hope of the gospel which has been proclaimed to every creature under heaven. No writing in the New Testament reflects more vividly the cosmic range of the story of Christ and, consequently, the awesome power of the hope of the gospel.

The variety apparent in these five documents makes all the more impressive the unanimity with which they witness to the centrality of the twin event of Christ's death and resurrection. They all find in that event a decisive disclosure of the mysteries of God's activity since creation, the related mysteries of Israel's election and of the biographies of all creatures. They all presuppose that the story form is the most appropriate way to show the connections between this event and other events. That story is comprehensive enough to cover God's whole work, yet detailed enough to cover each sparrow's fall. All five witnesses reflect the conviction that those connections are to be discerned in and through the vocation with which God's creative and redemptive purposes are accepted as the driving purposes of his servants. This is to say that each story poses a vision of the world that is inseparable from the vocation of God's people. To insert that story within the context of one's previous view of the world, or to translate it into the ordinary language indigenous to that ordinary world, is nothing less than a rejection of both vision and vocation. On the contrary, the story itself is an invitation for listeners to convert their previous visions of the world into *that* vision.[7] This conversion of visions, accomplished by the story, brings a simultaneous conversion of vocations. The new vocation is experienced from within the new world, the horizons of which are implicit in the story. The whole story becomes a metaphorical construct of which it becomes true to say: "When a metaphor contains a radically new vision of world it gives absolutely no information until after the hearer has entered into it and experienced it from inside itself."[8] "A true metaphor is one whose power creates the participation whereby its truth is experienced."[9]

The New Horizons

A new vision of the world—that is what is lacking in most treatments of the death and resurrection of Jesus. Normally we concern ourselves with accounts of a single event, isolated from its own horizons and inserted into ours. But to cope with radically different horizons boggles our minds, for we must do justice at once to vast panoramas of thought and to many precise details. It is not surprising that there are so few explorers in this realm, nor that their maps are so sketchy.

In the chapters which follow we cannot attempt to cover this whole terrain; we will examine only a few insets in the larger map, insets provided by a few specific texts. But because we have limited the scope of those later chapters, we feel obliged within the next few pages to provide a broad survey of New Testament thinking about that universe of which this event of death-resurrection is the center. Because of its condensed character, this survey will be difficult to read and even more difficult to assimilate. Some readers may prefer to turn immediately to the following chapter for a less compressed treatment of a specific text. Sooner or later, however, each of us needs to cope with the entire panorama of that world which comes into view through the New Testament witness as a whole. The following theses constitute an attempt to sketch such a panorama, to scan the wider horizoning of thought which was disclosed by this twin event. Because of space limitations, these theses cannot be defended here, but we believe there is ample evidence in the New Testament to support each of them.

I. Jesus' death and resurrection revealed the presence of God's active and powerful purpose.

   1. Because of this presence, the event never loses its character as a mystery. It hides God's purposes as well as dis-

closes them. It makes visible an activity which remains intrinsically invisible.

2. Because God's power becomes active in it, the event stands as a miraculous and spectacular sign, demonstrating the truth that what is impossible for men has become possible for God.

3. Ability to grasp what has happened presupposes on man's part a corresponding miracle, the healing of blind eyes and deaf ears. Involved is a radical change in all thinking about God, his wisdom and his power, his presence and his suffering.

II. The event discloses the character and import of God's other acts, from the creation of all things to their consummation.

1. It has an intrinsic capacity to enable men to grasp the purposes of God at the Alpha point, in creating mankind and in sealing covenants with his chosen people.

2. It has a similar capacity to show what God is about to do in fulfilling those covenants and in redeeming the whole of creation at the Omega point.

3. The implications of this event impel believers to change their ideas of what happens in creation and redemption, whether individual, communal or cosmic. Faith has the effect of reshaping all memories of God's previous work and all hopes for his subsequent work.

III. The event represented God's full approval of the vocation and work of his servant Jesus.

1. This vindication meant something first of all for Jesus himself. He had not been forsaken by his Father; rather had God established the work of his hands, "putting death forever behind him and life forever in front of him."[10]

2. The various terms for describing the event (anointing, etc.) agree in declaring that the Cross constituted the faithful completion of Jesus' earthly mission.

3. His vindication thereby came to serve as a judgment upon the sin and fears of both his enemies and his disciples.
4. Vindication of his mission also gave God's stamp of approval on Jesus' reinterpretations of Scripture, his liberation of people from sickness and from demons, his commands, threats, and promises.
5. Thereafter, disciples viewed the preresurrection traditions in postresurrection perspectives, and responded to the Risen Lord as he spoke with new authority through the earlier anecdotes.

IV. The exaltation of the Messiah coincided with the election of the messianic people.

1. The Passion Story revealed where the boundary lies between those who are "not my people" and those who are "my people" (Rom. 9:25–26). Pre-Golgotha conflicts continued, but their significance could now be seen.
2. This meant that conversion to Christ entailed change in previous attitudes toward Israel, as well as toward all other human communities.
3. New bonds between this Messiah and his people were reflected in the coincidence of many key images: head-body, Son-sons, King-kings, householder-stewards.
4. The vocation of Jesus became decisive in defining the vocation of his people. "Jesus' kerygma continues to be preached. . . . He still comes today with the same claim."[11]
5. The commands of Jesus now became the law of Christ, governing the internal and external behavior of his people.
6. "Life from the dead" is Paul's way of describing what will happen when Israel in the future turns from rejection of the Gospel to acceptance (Rom. 11:15). Paul's use of the term is flexible enough to apply to such a communal event.

V. In the exaltation of Jesus, the powerful presence of God's Spirit was made available to his people.

1. The descent of the Spirit in the resurrection was linked to the baptism of Jesus in the Jordan, giving continuity and coherence to Jesus' mission as a whole.
2. The same Spirit was present in commissioning the apostles, in the life given to the church at Pentecost, and in the baptism of every believer. "The imparting of the Spirit almost always means prophetic inspiration: a man is grasped by God who authorizes him to be his messenger."[12]
3. Having received the Spirit, each member of the church was empowered for multiple works of the Spirit, each work being a sign that pointed back to the resurrection and forward to the Parousia.
4. Discernment of the Spirit's presence was limited to those who had received the gift and who were engaged in those works. Faith itself was a gift of the Spirit, a prophetic witness to the resurrection.
5. Wherever the Spirit was at work, there the coming kingdom was penetrating the present age. "Life-in-the-Spirit is the life of the end of the ages."[13]

VI. The twin event was seen as a parable and a paradigm for the inner and outer experience of each follower.

1. In baptism the beginning of his new life was synchronized with his dying and rising with Christ.
2. His various duties as a follower became ways of dying daily, of bearing the Cross, commands of the Galilean Jesus which were clinched by the Calvary Jesus.
3. Dying with the Lord was seen as a death to the world, to the law, to sin, and to the self.[14]
4. Participation in worship on the Lord's Day and in intercessory prayer and action served to proclaim the Lord's death until his coming.
5. These correlations became intense in the experience of suffering and martydom; such suffering was seen as a precondition for full understanding of the Passion Story.
6. Thus the experience of each Christian itself became a

proclamation of the gospel, since he was "always being given up to death for Jesus' sake, so that the life of Jesus may be manifested" (2 Cor. 4:11).

VII. The various tasks of the community became forms by which it shared in the dying and rising of Christ.

1. Each celebration of the Eucharist proclaimed the defeat and victory of the Lord.
2. By worshiping the murdered Lamb rather than the murderous Dragon the church celebrated the power of the Lamb to create a new humanity, drawn from all races, nations, and languages (Rev. 5:9).
3. The daily life of the community was seen to reflect the same antithetical parallelisms used to describe what had happened in Jesus: weakness-power, folly-wisdom, death-life.
4. By its continual repentance and inner transformation the church participated in the universal condemnation and the universal forgiveness accomplished by God in Jesus' Passion.

VIII. The distinctive vocation of apostles was sealed in the twin event.

1. Here the Lord brought to completion their previous training: their understanding of Scripture, their insight into the necessity of suffering, their overcoming of fear, accepting the terms of their stewardship.
2. Here the Lord conveyed power to forgive sins, to heal the sick, to exorcize demons, to baptize converts, to govern churches.
3. The conferring of power was symbolized by the gift of the Spirit, the baptism of fire, the prophetic vision of divine activity. In various ways their work was linked to that of the Messiah as kings, priests, prophets, healers, teachers.
4. This event radically changed their self-image and their roles in the life of the messianic people.
5. One example of this fact is the conviction that the in-

tercessory life-giving of Jesus continued in the intercessory sufferings of the apostles, through which life and
glory accrued to others. (2 Cor. 1:6; 4:12–15; Eph. 3:13)

IX. The twin event enabled the apostles to reinterpret the
Scriptures.

1. It prompted typological treatments of the bondage in
   Egypt, the Exodus, the wilderness wanderings, the minis-
   try of Moses, the Exile, and the temple.
2. The Pentateuchal traditions, depicting God's covenants
   with Adam, Noah, and Abraham, became luminous as
   anticipations of the new covenant in Christ.
3. The liturgical traditions as imbedded in the psalms became newly resonant in the light of the suffering and
   glory of Christ.
4. "All the prophets" were now understood to have predicted the redemption in Christ and to anticipate as well
   the turmoil and joys of life within the Church.
5. Religious institutions were subjected to radical reevalua-
   tion in the light of the Passion. No institution retained any
   ultimate authority: priesthood or temple, circumcision or
   dietary laws, the Sabbath or the festivals.
6. Because Jesus had been crucified at the demands of religious leaders, his vindication represented "the fundamental and total crucifixion of all religion."[15]

X. Through Jesus God won a victory over the power of
Death itself.

1. Death was seen to be more than the act of dying; it was
   a cosmic power. "Among all the principalities and powers
   that influence or determine the course and life of nature
   and history, of society and the psyche, none appears to be
   so omnipotent, final and devastating as death."[16]
2. In his dying Jesus had been given the keys of Death and
   Hades, had become Lord of the dead as well as the living,
   had visited the spirits in prison. Through him others
   could share in that victory.
3. His movement from life to death, and from death to life,

signalled the beginning of the general resurrection and the final judgment of all the dead. No longer could the fact of dying separate any person from this Lord.

4. Faith in his resurrection produced a radical change in all definitions of both life and death, in conceptions of the power by which they claimed sovereignty over humanity.
5. Jesus' victory over death became available to believers who even before their own dying could share in his dying, and thus participate in final judgment and final grace (Rom. 8:9–11).
6. Thus new boundaries were set for each believer's vocation, a beginning and an "end" that determined the potential significance of each day's experience.

XI. Jesus' defeat-victory disclosed the subtle connections between the power of Death and the power of Sin and the Law.

1. The assurance of God's forgiveness in the resurrection enabled the penitent to be freed from the bondage which those powers had forged.
2. That release exploded in a vast range of signs of the new freedom: healings, exorcisms, gratitude, joy, love, praise.
3. Christ's victory over the power of Sin produced new definitions of what constitutes sin and righteousness.
4. Victory over the Law demolished the walls dividing Jew from Gentile, the alienation of male from female, rich from poor, master from slave. Though many communal problems emerged from this freedom, the way was opened for a society to be renewed from its center.[17]

XII. As the death of Jesus revealed the activity of invisible cosmic forces, his resurrection revealed a victory over them. These forces have various names: elemental spirits, rulers of this evil age, lordships and dominions, the Devil.

1. The victory of Jesus formed the climax to God's long struggle with the Devil, which had begun in Eden; at last the dragon had been defeated and his victims released from his bondage.
2. Faith in Christ's victory conveyed a knowledge of the

strategies of these invisible forces, freedom from fear of them, and power to defeat them whenever they attacked believer or church.

3. Their sovereignty had been proved by their power to inflict suffering; it was terminated by the voluntary acceptance of that suffering for the sake of others.

4. Freedom from these cosmic forces was coordinated with a change in ideas concerning their character and tenure, their relation to God and the world, to Israel and the nations.[18]

XIII. Through his victory over the powers Jesus had been given a name above every other name as King of kings and Lord of lords.

1. The power to name families on earth is the source of sovereignty for heavenly lords; the name given to Jesus indicated a shift in the balance of heavenly and earthly power.

2. This gave Jesus the right to name all the families of earth, to cancel former institutional ties, and to replace them in the new family.

3. To know Jesus' name was to know God's purposes, to live under his sovereignty, to have his power available, and to inherit his salvation.

4. All human actions and words could now be done in the name of Jesus; they could therefore embody his wisdom, grace, and strength. His humanity thus became the norm of what it is to be human.

XIV. Jesus' death and resurrection provided clues to the understanding of the traditional apocalyptic scenario, while that scenario in turn helped interpret that twin event.

1. The sufferings of the Messiah, of his messengers, of his messianic people became intelligible as the messianic woes.

2. Jesus' struggle with the Devil and his exorcism of demons became intelligible as episodes in the final conflict.

3. In his dying Jesus had descended into hell, had destroyed

hell's powers, liberated the spirits in prison, had shut up Satan in the abyss.

4. As a result, some Christians interpreted the present period as the millennial age separating the first from the second resurrections, the first and the final defeat of the evil powers (Rev. 20).

5. The Risen Lord provided continuity and coherence between the eschatological events in the past, present and future. All ideas of the future were personalized in terms of his presence.[19]

If, now, we return to our alphabetical shorthand, those symbols may help us summarize the changes in the horizons of Christian experience. In one respect, the death and resurrection of Jesus could be called the M-event, since it enabled believers to sense connections between each fragment of experience and the totality of things. Yet it would be better, I believe, to think of the church as preserving the same M-event as Israel: the Exodus, the leadership of the prophet Moses, the Sinai covenant, and the election as God's people. We should rather speak of Jesus' victory as the X-event, since it inaugurated the XYZ epoch in the fulfillment of God's covenant with Israel, and brought to a decisive close the CMX period. The apostles received a distinctive function, that of witnessing and revealing what had happened in this X-event, proclaiming it to unbelievers and teaching believers its paradigmatic relevance to their daily dilemmas. As a recipient of the Spirit, every follower of Christ lived within new vocational horizons, inasmuch as the X-event provided a vivid retrospect, and the Z-event a vivid prospect. The church as the community of the end-time was united by its common memory and this common hope; its corporate vocation had this beginning and this end. The language used by the church to describe the new situation was, of course, the everyday language of the common people, yet it became imbued with the prophetic Spirit appropriate for describing all that had happened in Jesus' mission and for expressing the eternal life of which the life in Christ is the first fruit.

Some Reflections

So much for a summary of the world-vision disclosed by this X-event. Such a summary betrays obvious deficiencies: it is too condensed to be lucid, too abstract to describe actual experience, too monochrome to suggest the diversities in thought and idiom. But it should at least suggest how vast and how pervasive was the transformation produced in the thinking and living of the ancient participants. Nor should we hastily limit the scope of those changes to internal psychic adjustments on the part of individuals. Christians were convinced that the death and resurrection of Jesus had in a mysterious but massive way changed the situation for every thing and every man. We may find such a conviction incredible; but that should not induce us to scoff at the intelligence of those believers or to impugn their integrity.

Readers may suppose that my effort to do justice to this perspective has been for the purpose of converting them to the Christian faith. Although my objective throughout has been exposition rather than conversion, it must be conceded that the preconditions for understanding are virtually identical with the preconditions for faith. I have already noted some of the credentials for interpreters who wish to understand why believers found in Jesus' death and resurrection an event that clarified their total human experience. Comprehension is built into the experience of listening to that story and into the subsequent response of repentance and faith. Comprehension of the character of this communal vocation is beyond the reach of those whose memories and hopes remain untouched by this God as he speaks through this Messiah and releases this Spirit. Every New Testament witness seems to assert that apart from some kind of parallel dying (whether in baptism or martyrdom, whether in relation to the Law or to the invisible rulers) no one can grasp the full significance of the Messiah's death. From first to last, some kind of correlation between *two* Passion stories appears to be a requisite for understanding the language of revelation. Interpreters who eliminate this requirement repudiate the evident desire of the original authors.

On the other hand, exegetes must not deceive themselves concerning the difficulties to be encountered when they begin to take those credentials seriously. It is easy to stipulate that interpreters must break loose from their own thought-world if they are to enter the world of such ancient witnesses as Peter. But we must recognize that there are great dangers in that stipulation. How can one shift worlds without sacrificing the integrity and independence of one's own thought-world? Can one avoid being dishonest with both himself and the audience? Will not the adopted perspective suffer from artificiality? We may grant, for example, that Peter and Paul actually participated in the sufferings of the Messiah and thereby could grasp the glory of his shame and the power of his weakness; yet can we without self-deception require that a modern scholar imitate Peter and Paul in this regard? If he puts on such a mask, will not his fellows rip it off? Another example: early Christians accepted the reality of a cosmic miracle without submitting an array of proofs of the kind which the modern skeptic requires. How can the latter accept without self-deception the cosmic miracles which the former presupposed? Does such a juggling of perspectives destroy the credibility of the interpreter? Even more, does it in fact destroy his sanity?

In this issue much more is at stake than the separate items of belief considered seriatim. The believer is expected to surrender forms and patterns of thinking which constitute the infrastructure of his mentality, a structure no less deeply ingrained for being the stamp of an atheistic culture. Can any person alter that infrastructure by thinking or wishing? Hans Frei has observed that whereas the biblical thought-world relied almost wholly on a narrative form to express its basic perceptions of reality, modern exegesis has ignored and destroyed that basic form, substituting for the realism of the ancient story either the historical facts which antedated the creation of that story or the conceptualized meanings conveyed by it.[20] As a result of this substitution the biblical apprehensions have become quite inaccessible to us. But to recognize this fact poses an acute problem: can any modern interpreter, without doing violence to his own mind, recapture and utilize this ancient narrative form as disclosing the structure of the world in which he actually lives?

The story form seems particularly inappropriate to us in dealing with cosmic and/or ontic reality. Biblical cosmology (or is it an anticosmology?) includes attitudes which our cosmology excludes, and the cosmology that is native to us and to our age cannot be readily laid aside. A biblical writer could make serious metaphorical reference to the "darkness at noon" (Mk. 15:33); when we do so we sound either silly or pretentious rather than profound. Poets may help us, but can we take their cosmological notions seriously?

> This world is not conclusion;
> A sequel stands beyond,
> Invisible, as music,
> But positive, as sound.
> It beckons and it baffles;
> Philosophies don't know.
>
> And through a riddle, at the last,
> Sagacity must go.
> To guess it puzzles scholars;
> To gain it, men have shown
> Contempt of generations,
> And crucifixion known.[21]

The crucifixion of intellect is precisely what many biblical scholars fear most. Nowhere is that "crucifixion" more feared than at the point where the two cosmologies, ancient and modern, collide. Consider our response to the ancient witnesses concerning the eschatological significance of the death-resurrection of Jesus. Those witnesses saw the event as an X-event initiating a process that would rapidly move through Y to Z. The release of the gifts of the Holy Spirit—faith, hope, love—was a sign that what had happened would soon be completed in the return of the Messiah. It needs no argument to support the contention that modern attitudes toward the world automatically exclude such conceptions of the p/f component. It seems utterly impossible for modern interpreters to view the X-event as having genuine *cosmological* significance for us. The nineteen centuries that have passed since the X of this story have effectively broken any direct connection between the X and the Z. For the modern exegete to reaffirm the apostolic revelation would make him as foreign to his world as a UFO.

In saying this we have, of course, also indicated a limited kinship between the modern academy and the original audience of Peter in Acts 3. That audience instinctively inserted Peter's story into the context of its own world-view and as a result the murder of Jesus had seemed to them a perfectly logical expression of an inherited conception of the p/f component and of a traditional CMX. Peter's witness to God's act in raising Jesus (you killed him . . . God raised him . . . we are witnesses) and his call to repentance represented in effect the reverse possibility: they should insert their former story into this *new* context. If, as he said, their act had not been righteousness but murder, their whole previous world-view, from beginning to end, from center to circumference, must be discarded as false. The collision between Peter's cosmology and theirs was comparable to the collision between his and ours. At the very least, honesty compels us to recognize the seriousness of that collision. How shall we deal with it?

It is because I believe that this conflict of cosmologies represents the nub of modern misunderstandings of the gospel story that I will devote the remainder of this book to the exegesis of four specific texts. The first deals with the paradigmatic power of Christ's cross, as an X-event, to include the crucifixion of the world; the second with the cosmic vocation of the church during the period between X and Z; the third with the presence of Christ in his church during that period; and the fourth with a prophetic vision of the end of the world, the Z-event.

3
The Crucifixion of the World
Galatians 6:14–15

*So Paul was a jail-bird and a fantast
who acted out a new apocalypse*
. . . .
*a scene-changer and a world-changer,
an underground man with his guerilla troupe,
and a poster-artist
by whom Jesus Christ was "publicly placarded
as crucified."*[1]

In the preceding chapter we focused attention on three clauses
in a sermon attributed to Peter, his call for repentance and
faith issued to his Jewish brothers. Those three clauses centered on two related actions: the murder of the Messiah and
his vindication. Those two actions were seen by Peter, as well
as by other New Testament writers, as marking a decisive
break with the old and a decisive emergence of the new. Their
vocation was understood as the consequence of union with
Christ in that event. But such a union meant that the measure
of their faith would be the degree to which they shared in that
decisive break between old and new. Their acceptance of Jesus
as God's Son meant that his death and resurrection became
the X-event which determined for them the meaning of all
subsequent events.[2]

In reflecting upon the multiple ways by which New Testament writers described that event, I have concluded that the

most stubborn barrier between them and us lies in our vastly different conceptions of space and time. Our conceptions form molds into which we force all ideas about our experiences. Nothing is so resistant to change as those conceptions, since they form the infrastructure of all our thinking. So when things happen which defy those molds, our instinct is to force the new event into our old understandings of the world, rather than to change the infrastructure to conform to the new experience. This is what happens when the biblical witness to Jesus' death and resurrection conflicts with our cosmology; we doubt whether that twin event has had any discernible effect upon the world as we know it.

This tendency is exemplified in our reactions, whether instinctive or informed, to the triple crucifixion mentioned by Paul in Galatians 6:14:

> Far be it from me to glory except in the cross of our Lord Jesus Christ, by which the world has been crucified to me, and I to the world.[3]

The Second Crucifixion

We have just spoken of the triple crucifixion found in this verse, as if a single event were in Paul's mind. That is clearly his intent: in the one cross three crucifixions took place. The first—the crucifixion of Jesus—seems to refer directly to an historical event, the actuality of which is not seriously in doubt. Without much hesitation we can share the assertion of the creed: "suffered under Pontius Pilate, crucified, dead and buried." Inasmuch as this is an historical event, the historian's verdict must be respected. In this case belief seems to be founded on fact.

Then we may ask how we react to Paul's assertion that he had himself been crucified to the world? This, too, appears, on the face of things, entirely credible, for it seems to refer primarily to a psychic experience about which Paul would know more than anyone else. The statement refers to a subjective upheaval in his attitudes toward the world, a conversion of

values which produced a new ego structure. He was no longer
dependent on the world for the realization of his desires. Because such upheavals belong to the realm studied by psycholo-
gists, it is they who are qualified to offer other explanations of
the same phenomenon; yet they are hardly entitled to deny
that some change, more or less radical, had surfaced in Paul's
subjective relation to the world. The true character of that
change may remain obscure, for it took place in the caverns of
Paul's soul, but most of us are inclined to accept the fact of
actual change in his conscious vocation.

But when we ask about the other crucifixion, our reaction is
subtly but strikingly different: "The world has been crucified
to me." Does that assertion make any sense? If so, what sense?
Is the assertion credible? Paul contends that in the crucifixion
of Christ decisive changes have also taken place in the world.
But which world is this? And how has it been changed? Our
confusion is due in part to uncertainties as to which authorities
are qualified to judge this claim. Should we expect an historian, an Arnold Toynbee, to determine whether the world has
in fact been changed? Or a physicist, perhaps the latest Nobel
laureate? Or a journalist, a Harry Reasoner? Or does Every-
man carry with him a map of the cosmos that enables him to
judge the truth of Paul's rhetoric? We could say, "Cosmology
is no part of the message of the Gospel."[4] At the other extreme, we could say that according to Paul the crucifixion of
Christ produced changes in the cosmos that require the interpreter to die to his previous conceptions of what the universe
is like. Much is therefore at stake in the exegesis of this verse.
On what terms can we understand Paul's assertion? On what
terms believe it to be true?

Let us first attend to the immediate implications of the assertion itself. The whole sentence constitutes a single unit of
thought. Its explosive exclamation, "Far be it from me," is
Paul's effort to place the strongest possible emphasis on what
follows. For Paul all other issues of thought and action can be
telescoped into this issue: in what does a person glory? Paul
locates the ground and object of his own trust, his glorying,

his rejoicing, his enthusiasm, in the cross of his Lord. This is the primary reference that must be kept firmly in mind. His theology is a theology of the cross; and if Galatians be selected as the Magna Carta of that theology, this verse becomes the most impassioned proclamation of that Magna Carta. It is clear that, although Paul speaks only of himself in the verse, he implies that what he says should apply without diminished emphasis to every other follower of this Lord.

Of the three crucifixions cited, the last two are clearly made secondary to the first. It is in and by the cross of Christ that the world and the self have been crucified. We should notice the fact that the verb is in the passive voice: the two subjects have been acted upon from outside themselves, have been subjected to forces greater than their own, forces that have produced changes commensurate with crucifixion. The subjects have not themselves initiated or desired those changes. One does not crucify himself. Who, then, crucified the world? Two possibilities appear: either Jesus, the Crucified, since the prepositional phrase "by which" may be translated "by whom," or the God of Jesus, in obedience to whom Jesus accepted death. We should also notice that the verb is in the perfect tense. The radical alteration has been accomplished presumably at the same time as Jesus' crucifixion; yet that alteration continues to determine and to dominate the present situation. The change is permanent. The present position of both the self and the world continues to be that of having been crucified. To glory in the cross of Christ means that Paul continues to live as a crucified man in a crucified world.

We must suppose that Paul intended to create a precise balance between these two derived crucifixions: the world has been crucified to me, I have been crucified to the world. These two are separable, yet interdependent. Neither can be fully understood alone; neither can be telescoped into the other. In both cases the matter under consideration is a relationship: the world is viewed in its relation to Paul, Paul is viewed in his relation to the world. It is this double relationship that has suffered radical change. We have observed how in Acts 3:15

the three actions of three subjects (you . . . God . . . we) intersected in the cross of Jesus. Again here in Galatians we encounter three subjects: Jesus, the world, I. Here again the three stories converge in a common center, the cross of Jesus. This fusion of centers has produced a fusion of horizons; the three subjects now have a common past and a common future; their memories and hopes, heretofore separate, are unified by the interlocking crucifixions: Christ, the world, the self. Christ is understood only in his relation to the world and the self; the self is understood only in its relation to Christ and the world; and last of all the world is understood only in its relation to Christ and the self. This triangle ceases to exist if any of its three sides is ignored. All three share in a common end and a common beginning.

This being true, we need to recover as precisely as possible what was Paul's conception of this world and the method of its crucifixion. Such an objective would, of course, be unnecessary if Paul's statement had originally functioned simply as a wild rhetorical flourish, having no genuine substance. There are those who are tempted to accept this solution. But if that had been the case, Paul's argument in the letter as a whole would have been fatally weakened. He was not engaged in building sand castles, but in trying to convince some very stubborn opponents who were quite eager to spot rhetorical nonsense. The whole Epistle is a carefully mounted polemic against these adversaries. One point at issue was precisely the differing attitudes toward this cosmos. Paul wanted to make his assertion concerning its crucifixion intelligible to them. Their perceptions of this cosmos did not as yet coincide with his, so his whole intent was to persuade them to adopt his position and to "walk by this rule" (6:16), recognizing the full scope of the new creation. If the Epistle itself is evidence that these opponents were baffled by Paul's thought on this point (we are surely not the first to be confused), it is also evidence that he believed in the strategic importance of clarifying this point.

The statement that this particular world has been crucified

immediately excludes several of the possible definitions of cosmos. Did Paul have in mind the physical universe, the heavens and the earth, the sum total of created things? No, that denotation cannot be inserted into this context. Did he refer to the earth as the home of mankind, the fixed stage on which all the dramas of history are enacted? That notion is equally foreign. So, too, we can exclude a comprehensive reference to humanity, to all the inhabitants of the earth, Jews and Gentiles, men, women, and children. None of these three magnitudes fits the thought of this verse. If by cosmology we mean objective scientific knowledge of such matters as these, it follows that this verse has little if any cosmological weight. In any case, we should eliminate these conceptions of the world from consideration here.

However, the lexicon supplies still another definition of cosmos, one that is a bit more congenial to our text: the world is coextensive with the present evil age, that realm of sin and death which is ruled by invisible powers. Of the major options in the dictionary, this alone approaches the tenor of Paul's thought. But while this definition may be adequate in other Pauline passages, it is rather awkward in this one. It is difficult to speak naturally and realistically of the crucifixion of *that* entity through the cross of Christ. Our study of Galatians 6:14 will follow sounder procedure if we move from text to inference, shaping our idea of world to fit this particular argument. This verse itself seems to suggest at least three features:

1. This cosmos is of such a nature as to embody a structure of relations to individual persons ("to me" . . . "I to it").
2. This structure of relations is of such a nature as to be vulnerable to sudden violent termination (crucified).
3. This termination has actually happened in the cross of Christ, though this actuality can readily be ignored or denied, as was the case with some Galatian believers.

Keeping those points in mind, let us see what inferences other verses in Galatians may suggest concerning the character of this world which has been crucified to Paul.

— From 6:13–14 we infer that this world is a realm where people glory "in the flesh." So whenever they substitute the cross of Christ as the occasion and object of glorying, they provide evidence that this world has been crucified.

— From 6:15 we infer that this world is a realm where such distinctions as those between circumcision and uncircumcision are accorded great weight. So whenever such distinctions cease to count, that particular world has been crucified and has been replaced by a new creation.

— From 6:12–13 we infer that this world is a realm where devout people give top priority to God's Law even though they are unable to keep that Law. So whenever the authority of that Law loses its priority, that particular world has been crucified.

- From 5:11; 6:12, 17 we infer that this world is a realm where people are encouraged and trained to avoid suffering and death, in this case persecution for the sake of Christ. Whenever that system of values has been changed by the voluntary acceptance of death, that particular world has been crucified.

— From 5:16–24; 6:8 we infer that this world is a realm where the desires of the flesh produce the works of the flesh, and where, accordingly, people in seeking to avoid corruption are corrupted. Whenever people overcome those desires and renounce those works they show that this particular world has been crucified. In this context any misuse of the term *flesh* guarantees a mistaken conception of the term *world*.

— From 5:16, 21; 6:2, 15 we infer that this world is a realm that stands in opposition to the new creation, so that the two are mutually exclusive. Whenever people enter God's kingdom, submit to Christ's law and walk by the Spirit, they give their witness to the crucifixion of this world.

— From 4:21–31 we infer that this world is a space inhabited by an ancestral covenantal community, variously described as the present Jerusalem, the descendants of Hagar, successive generations of slaves. Whenever God

seals a new covenant with a new community, that world
has been crucified.
— From 3:23–28 we infer that this world is a realm where
sharp distinctions between races, classes, and sexes have
been established by religious rules and enforced by religious sanctions. Whenever those distinctions have ceased
to carry weight, that world has been crucified.
— From 4:1–10 we infer that this world is constituted by the
effective sovereignty of elemental spirits *(stoicheia)* whose
power operates through many types of religious behavior, but especially through the observance of sacred times
and seasons. Whenever a community is freed from that
sovereignty by the knowledge of the true God, that particular world has been crucified.

If one now combines those nine inferences into the description of a single reality, he will see that this reality is so powerful
and massive that the term *world* becomes entirely fitting. This
reality is as ordered and as coercive as the systems of law and
custom that regulate society. It is as persistent as the linguistic
and ethnic groups that preserve their separate identity and
avoid assimilation for century after century. It is as pervasive
as dominant standards of wealth, wisdom, and nobility that
fuel social ambitions and inflame social animosities. It is as
elemental as the division of time into weeks, and as the tendency to punctuate the year with sacred holidays. It is as universal as the craving for security and health. It is as deeply rooted
as the habitual discrimination between one sex and another,
one class and another. Its inhabitants have every reason to
assume its indestructibility, ignoring the degree to which its
longevity depends upon that very acceptance. At every point
we must recognize the religious character of this reality: it is
grounded in ancient religious traditions, structured by perennial religious needs, expressed in deeply rooted pieties and
loyalties. Liberation from this world requires

being liberated from fear for oneself, no longer to adapt oneself to this society, its idols and taboos, its imaginary enemies
and fetishes; and in the name of him who was once the victim
of religion, society and the state, to enter into solidarity with
the victims of religion, society and state.[5]

So we must conclude that whenever this world, this cosmos,
is mentioned in Galatians, one needs to recall the ways, highly
subtle but highly effective, by which the *stoicheia* establish and
retain control over religious communities. It is with their
power that Paul is concerned. Since they owe that power to a
particular structure of human relations, they had been crucified when that structure had been "nailed to the cross" of
Christ (Col. 2:14). There their power had been terminated, yet
these *stoicheia* display precisely those qualities of permanence
which induced Galatian Christians to act as if they had not
been crucified, especially with regard to such an important
matter as the pivotal distinction between Jew and Gentile: the
cultic and moral requirement of circumcision. On that matter,
these elemental spirits continued to claim the full support of
such covenantal bonds as had been described in Genesis 17.

Whenever Galatian believers bowed to the authority of
those bonds, they became blind servants of the *stoicheia*, but
whenever they refused such conformity, these gods became
no-gods. This may sound as if the death of these gods were a
matter of individual decision, and there is a degree of truth in
that view. We may, in fact, have encouraged this conclusion in
our summary by using the formula, "whenever . . . that particular world has been crucified." But this formula is misleading.
To be sure, the mark of change in the existence of the believer
is his present freedom and his acceptance of persecution, and
such freedom always emerges at the point where a person
makes his own decision. Yet Paul insisted that this decision had
become possible and imperative only because the world had
already been crucified through the freedom and persecution
of Jesus. This point has been fully established in a noteworthy
study by R. C. Tannehill:

The individual is unable to free himself by himself. Only God's eschatological act, an act by which the old world is invaded and a new life in a new world is created, can free man from his slavery. Such an act involves the old world and new world as wholes.[6]

That most decisive of all revolutions had been accomplished in the death of Jesus. Even so, that revolution must be accompanied by and manifested in the action of his followers. It was in fact possible for the Galatian adversaries to relapse from this freedom into a new slavery to the *stoicheia*. They had so relapsed; having begun with the Spirit they were ending with the flesh (3:3). Judging by their action, Christ had "died to no purpose" (2:21). That very apostasy, however, made all the more decisive that past action of Christ. His death had once for all demonstrated the weakness and poverty of those elemental spirits. The prestige of this whole world had been destroyed (4:9). Indeed the finality and the present potency of this previous crucifixion of the world furnished the hinge on which Paul's argument turned. If he were wrong on this point, then he would be forced to concede the rightness of his adversaries on many other points.

As we have noticed, the verb he used is the perfect passive: "has been crucified." In this context, the presence of metaphorical thinking is obvious: the world did not hang on a cross, subject to brutal violence of that sort. Yet it would be wrong to downgrade the far-reaching effects of that event: when Christ was crucified, this particular world had been put to death. Its rulers had lost their power, wisdom, glory, and longevity. The cross of Christ had clarified the relative strength and tenure of the opposing sovereignties, God versus these no-gods. So when we deal with these two crucifixions, of Christ and of this world, we do not deal with two events, separated by a stretch of linear time, but with one event that incorporates within itself that stretch of time, however short or long.

Other passages in Paul's letters provide analogous ways of

setting forth what had happened in this same event. For example, we learn from chapters 1 and 2 of First Corinthians that something had happened to the wisdom of these rulers of the world. To them the cross had proved Jesus' folly; in God's truth it had disproved their wisdom. If they had known the truth, they would not have crucified the Lord of glory (2:8). To them the cross had demonstrated Jesus' weakness; in God's truth it had set the boundary of their power. That was the place where God's weakness had proved stronger than the entrenched power of the world (1:18–25). It had demolished the structures of glory by which that world is supported. The continued power of the world depended upon its triple threat: the power of the Law, of sin, of death. The crucified Jesus had destroyed that triple threat (1 Cor. 15:51–57). Paul had detected in the death of Jesus the operating presence of "every rule and every authority and power" (surely including the *cosmos* of Gal. 6:14 and the *stoicheia* of Gal. 4:3); he therefore had seen in the victory of Jesus their crucifixion on that very cross (1 Cor. 15:24–28). Viewed from this perspective, the crucifixion of this world is simply one dramatic way of describing the transfer in that balance of power that had been accomplished in the death of Christ. Like every other pivot in Paul's thinking, his conception of the world and its times had been redefined by that transfer. Nothing at all lay outside the range of Christ's victory: death, life, angels, principalities, things present, things to come, height, depth (Rom. 8:38–39). It is deceptively easy but surely false to diminish the range and force of such declarations.

All this is simply to say, in our shorthand language, that with this X-event the believer dates the beginning of the new creation in all its scope and energy (Gal. 6:15). Paul's Galatian adversaries had underestimated or ignored that beginning; it ill behooves the interpreter of Paul to follow their example. Any interpreter who is interested in Paul's own thought must do full justice to such assertions as these:

— One has died for all, therefore *all* have died. (2 Cor. 5:14)
— If any one is in Christ, a *new* creation. (2 Cor. 5:17)

— God was in Christ reconciling *the world* to himself. (2 Cor. 5:19)

— He disarmed the principalities and powers and made a public example of them, *triumphing over them* in the cross. (Col. 2:15)

— He has delivered us from the *dominion of darkness* and transferred us to the kingdom of his beloved Son. (Col. 1:13)

— At the name of Jesus every knee should bow, *in heaven* and on earth and *under the earth.* (Phil. 2:10)

— God made him sit at his right hand in the heavenly places, far above *all rule and authority and power and dominion.* (Eph. 1:21)

— He has broken down the dividing wall of hostility by abolishing in his flesh *the law.* (Eph. 2:14–15)

— Through the cross he killed *the enmity* in himself. (Eph. 2:16)

— When he ascended on high he led *a host of captives* (or, he took captivity captive). (Eph. 4:8)

We note that in these quotations Paul used various verbs to mark the victory of Christ over the *stoicheia* of the world. Only in Galatians 6:14 did he say that a particular world had been crucified on Christ's cross. But elsewhere the verbs leave no doubt of an equally decisive victory over the hostile powers. These other verses ratify our emphasis on the perfect passive in Gal. 6:14, "the world has been crucified to me." On the cross Christ had terminated the world's authority over "me."

We need now to scrutinize the role of that personal pronoun in Paul's thinking. How are we to understand the "to me"?

1. It surely presents Paul as a representative case. He assumes that what he says could and should be said of every Christian.

2. It excludes the possibility that Paul himself had crucified the world.

3. "To me" in this context is not properly construed to mean "in my view of things" or "as I see the world, it has been crucified."

To be sure, the whole of this sentence and the extended argument of which it is a part presupposes the standpoint of faith. In this sentence, however, "to me" clearly refers to the whole fabric of relationships of the self to the world. The dative case has the same force here as in the next clause "to the world," which surely does not mean "in the world's view of things." The world's authority over me has been terminated, just as my loyalty to it has been terminated. There is a two-sided breach in the previous relationship, a breach made possible by a change in both parties. The direct result of this breach is a person's freedom and his persecution, neither of which would transpire unless the authority of the world had in fact been broken. It is the world that takes the initiative in using persecution whenever its power is challenged. "Only if there is a new world is the individual in a position to exist in a new way."[7]

The Third Crucifixion

So far we have concentrated upon the second crucifixion. Paul also wrote about a third: "I have been crucified to the world." We should now ask whether this third death throws any new light upon the second. The same perfect passive form of the verb indicates that the action has been done "to me" in the past in such a way as to alter the present situation. A two-way bond of mutual interaction has been broken; to call a person a Christian is to speak of him as having been crucified.[8] How does this event affect the world? The first step in analysis must be to deny that the two clauses are interchangeable. Paul's death to the world is not the same thing as the world's death to him; otherwise the two statements could be collapsed into one, the death of one self in the birth of another. Since, however, this death of the self is a frequent Pauline metaphor, we should not ignore its harsh actuality.

Already in Galatians (2:19–20) Paul has spoken of this death in quite realistic terms: "I through the law died to the law." This is strikingly similar to our verse in 6:14. The law represents the *stoicheia* in their oppressive hold upon members of Israel: to die to that aspect of the law parallels the death to the world. In this case, we note the added comment: it was *through the law* that Paul had died to the law. *This* form of crucifixion had paradoxically both confirmed and demolished the law. Similar implications may be noticed elsewhere; Paul speaks of dying with Christ in baptism, of bearing about in one's body the dying of Jesus, of a person's death to sin, to the flesh, to the law, and even to death. The very frequency of these metaphors dulls our sensitivity to the radical intent of the words. In each case, however, Paul intends a rugged realism; e.g., death to sin is every whit as difficult and as decisive as crucifixion to the world. Yet exegetes have almost uniformly reduced Paul's thought to a dimension of banal moralism. For example, G.S. Duncan:

> All the things in life which to the natural man are imposing and attractive have lost significance for him—they have become dead things.[9]

That observation is of course true, but it is too bland to do justice to Galatians 6:14. In a similar way, J. H. Ropes concludes that "Paul has become detached from every worldly aim."[10] Such quiet dampening of Pauline dynamite is encouraged by the most influential of the Greek-English lexicons, in which our verse is translated in such a way as to destroy its carefully crafted parallelism: "The world has been crucified for [sic] me, and I have been crucified to [sic] the world."[11] The same tendency may be observed on the part of that master exegete, Rudolf Bultmann. His existentialism helps him to do greater justice to the radical transformation of the individual believer, but it prevents him from coping with Paul's stress on a corresponding transformation of the world. Bultmann writes:

> To them 'the world' is crucified on the cross of Christ and they to it (Gal. 6:14). For them the elemental spirits of the 'kosmos' to which they were once enslaved have been unmasked as the 'weak and beggarly elemental spirits' (Gal. 4:9). Therefore they will some day be judges over the world

(1 Cor. 6:2ff.). All this is true because, in point of fact, they have become new persons.[12]

Note that Professor Bultmann has shifted the phrase "to them" to the beginning of the sentence, thereby reducing the crucifixion of the world to a private subjective attitude. That is also the implication of the "for them" of the second sentence. A similar effect is produced by putting into inverted commas both "the world" and "kosmos"; in doing this he warns the reader not to take these words in any public or objective sense. So, too, when he says that the persons have become new "in point of fact," he implies that the same degree of factual change does *not* take place in the case of "the world." He illustrates similar caution by postponing to some undefined date in the future the Christians' judgeship over the world (1 Cor. 6:1–8). Throughout this exegesis we discern a refusal to concede to the cross any power to change the world; its impact is limited to changes far short of any genuine crucifixion. It would seem that to Professor Bultmann Paul's assertion about the world was neither intelligible nor credible; in this respect he is fully representative of contemporary exegesis.[13]

I do not wish my protest to be misunderstood. I am not interested in attacking colleagues but in clarifying Paul's perspective. Bultmann must be credited with recovering the full realism of Paul's crucifixion to the world; he is less successful in dealing with Paul's equally radical idea of the world's crucifixion to Paul. When interpreters reduce the dimensions of Paul's thought to moralistic or existentialist changes, they betray a kinship with Paul's adversaries in Galatia who could not fathom any substantial change in the power of the *stoicheia*. That was the nub of the issue in the Galatian churches.

Why should there be such a chasm between Paul's mind and our own in this matter? For one thing, where we think of the separateness of the two categories, objective and subjective, Paul thought in terms of their interrelatedness: the world to me, I to the world. We tend to think of both the self and the world as self-enclosed and separate entities without defining them in their relation to a common origin in the same creation. Paul could think of them only as created, sustained, and judged by God. Because all things have been created by God, any new creation must involve both self and world simultaneously. If God has declared the elemental spirits of the world to be weak and beggarly, then we must accept that as their true status. Unless this be granted, the scope of the new creation in Galatians 6:15 is arbitrarily limited to the emotional life of believers; this would constitute a tacit denial of any new creation. Paul's thought presupposes a conception of the world in which the conflicting activities of God and the *stoicheia* are definitive. Our cosmologies virtually exclude such a presupposition. And so our religion becomes unrelated to our "world"; by contrast Paul's "world" was related at every point to his faith.[14]

Another chasm between the two cosmologies consists of our conception of linear time. That conception induces us to remove Christ's death from us by long centuries, for we quite automatically locate that event at a specific point on our timeline. In fact, we can conceive of God's action only as an intervention in what we call time, which thereafter runs along at the same speed and in the same direction as before the intervention. So we cannot grant that in Christ's crucifixion something happened to time. The very idea of a new creation requires a different perspective:

> God does not act *in* history or intervene *in* time. It is the presence of God which, in calling to us for response, creates our history and gives us time, this history and this time. Time is, in both senses, the present of God.[15]

It is, of course, possible to argue with G. Schneider that this new creation refers only to "a supernatural transformation within the Christian's soul."[16] But that interpretation seems to deny either that God is the creator of the world or that he has disclosed his creative power and wisdom in the cross of Christ. Much more adequate is the insistence of P. Stuhlmacher that only a fully ontological exegesis can do justice to this strand of Pauline thought.[17]

Freedom and Persecution

What kind of ontological thinking is required by Paul's argument in Galatians? What kind will do justice to both objective and subjective components in what God has done on the cross of Christ? Here we may find help by examining again the nine inferences (above, p. 83) concerning the cosmos that has been crucified. The greatest common denominator in these nine inferences is the role of God's Law with respect to the covenant community. The Law prescribes the importance of the flesh, the distinctions between circumcision and uncircumcision (e.g., Gen. 17), and the ancestral distinctions between sexes, classes, races, and religions. The Law detects in the cross a sin, a folly, a weakness that precludes faith. The Law establishes fixed boundaries around the covenantal community, boundaries that operate in such a way as to encourage a glorying in the flesh, in the desires and the deeds of the flesh. In short, the Law has become one of "the elemental spirits of the cosmos" which has kept its obedient servants in a condition of bondage, a bondage made all the more complete by its sacralizing of social customs and rules. It is *this* Law that had been crucified to Paul, and Paul to this Law (2:19–20). When one seeks to do justice to the manifest authority exercised by this Law, it becomes absurd to deny to this "world" genuine ontological status. Man's pre-Golgotha existence is defined by the Law's authority over him, an authority which he accepts as mediating God's own authority. When that authority over God's creation is terminated, the world that is governed by that Law is crucified to God's people and a new creation is born. From this standpoint (i.e., that of the Law) the crucifixion of *this* world to Paul formed an essential twin to the crucifixion of Paul to this world. The authority of the world over Paul had to be broken before this slave could declare his freedom from that authority.

It is true, of course, that to be free this slave had to be crucified to the world if he were to be included in the new creation. Freedom is authentic only as *his* freedom from the *stoicheia* of his world. Why, then, did Paul decide to glory *only* in the cross? Because in that cross he was given the freedom of the new creation, entailing simultaneously the death of the authority of those *stoicheia* and the death of his own subservience to their authority. His conversational partners could not glory in the cross alone because they did not recognize the same triple crucifixion. In short, they had not yet accepted the freedom from religion which the cross of Christ had won for them. Their fear of this cross-given freedom meant that it was impossible for them to grasp the full scope of the new creation or the new definition of the "Israel of God," impossible for them to live by the Spirit or to fulfil the law of Christ (5:14–15). Such things remained outside the horizons of everyone to whom the world had not been crucified by Christ's cross.

In Galatians Paul selected, along with freedom, a second sign that this triple crucifixion had taken place, a sign embracing both objective and subjective actualities. He has been persecuted; he bears in his body the scars of that persecution (6:17). Not only is this the mark of his freedom; it is present evidence that the triple crucifixion of 6:14 has indeed taken place. His adversaries, by contrast, have succeeded in avoiding that persecution. Paul sees their avoidance as a measure of their continued bondage to the *stoicheia,* and hence as good evidence of their refusal to recognize that new creation, the Israel of God, which had been introduced by the triple crucifixion. The reality of this persecution fully justifies the choice of crucifixion as the metaphor governing 6:14. We conclude, then, that this verse becomes an incomparable epitome of the Gospel. But that Gospel would have evaporated into fog if the Law-enslaving world had not in fact been crucified in the cross of Jesus.

Even though Paul wanted his readers to see the tragic results of their slavery to the Law, a good case can be advanced to support the position of his antagonists. By the same token, one should not underestimate the liberating results of adopting his position. If the historicality of Christ's death and the historicality of the believers' death are supported and accompanied by the historicality of the world's crucifixion, then believers have indeed been freed. But if the world (in the sense given) has not been crucified, then liberation remains an impossible dream and humanity remains doomed to perpetual servitude. But if the world has in fact been crucified, citizens of the new creation enter a story that is pervaded by peace and mercy (6:16).

We should make a distinction between Paul's position and two alternative ones. One position is that of those liberation movements that suppose that freedom is impossible until social reform has destroyed the authority of existing social institutions. A second is the position of those who expect freedom to emerge only from a subjective change in the attitude of persons toward those institutions (e.g., the Law). Paul differed from both by insisting that both objective and subjective changes had already been accomplished by Christ. He celebrated freedom as a gift of God made actual in that event. He believed that a refusal to live in terms of those three crucifixions meant that "Christ had died to no purpose." For a community to live within the context of those crucifixions was to accept and to manifest the new creation. Paul viewed an uncrucified world as a place of unbroken bondage, and a crucified world as a doorway to glorious unprecedented freedom. One is a way of describing cosmic slavery to the body of sin and death (Rom. 7:24), the other a way of confessing the mysterious and miraculous freedom in the body of Christ. One is the worst of all conceivable situations, the other is the best, even though (or precisely because) its price is persecution and crucifixion.

It is not easy for a modern reader to grasp the multiple dimensions of freedom in the body of Christ. Some of these dimensions are disclosed in Galatians: liberation from the religious illusions that are embodied in rites of initiation and in routines of celebration (the cherished "proofs" of belonging to an elect community); liberation from fears of ostracism, failure, and death; liberation from the restraints exercised by cosmic and communal "law and order." In tracing those dimensions, one can easily get drunk on the elixir of one's own verbosity. But a dose of persecution quickly takes care of that! It forces a person to translate the glittering generality of freedom into "the marks of Jesus" (Gal. 6:17), and that translation in Paul's case may have been more persuasive that his verbal arguments.

Another type of translation may be observed in the case of one of Paul's converts, Onesimus. That translation, which can be traced between the lines of the Epistle to Philemon, has been overlooked in many "theologies of liberation." If we retrace the story of Onesimus we discover a dramatic sequence of experiences of captivity and liberation. In Act I we glimpse Onesimus as a slave, presumably in the household of Philemon. After carefully laying plans for escape, he made his escape good and no doubt relished the newly won emancipation. In Act II we glimpse Onesimus captured and thrown into prison, his "paradise lost," but in prison he encounters the apostle and becomes a slave of Jesus the Messiah. In rapid succession he had experienced three types of captivity (to Philemon, to a Roman prison, to the crucified Jesus) and two types of liberation.

In Act III, for reasons unknown to us, Onesimus was freed from prison, and for reasons better known Paul remained under confinement, though both men now had become free in Christ. What happened? With Paul's approval, if not urging, Onesimus returns to "square one," to his former master Philemon, taking with him Paul's letter requesting that the master receive back his slave, now as a brother, and requesting also that Onesimus be sent back to Paul to provide help in the name of Philemon.

Act IV would represent Philemon's response—which is something hidden in the mists of history. Assuming his consent to Paul's request, the three men in Christ—Philemon, Onesimus, Paul—would each exemplify a captivity stronger than all others and a freedom born of that captivity transcending all lesser, mundane liberties. Onesimus represents Pauline theology in action; more important even than that, he demonstrates the power of Christ to free a person from every other type of captivity.

Some Implications

We may well ask how many American congregations can represent that theology, can demonstrate that power. One answer comes when we ask: do they live in bondage to law or in the freedom of those for whom the law has died and who have died to the law? To this question the first option is surely the truer one. In a recent Bible study series which I conducted in Connecticut for laymen from four different parishes and denominations, I found not a single person ready to engage in actions of civil disobedience because of his faith and not a single congregation which would support such a member. It would be impossible for such a group (twenty-five lay persons) either to understand or to share Paul's statement "I died to the law that I might live to God" (2:19) or to view the cross on the altar as a sign of the world's (the law's) crucifixion to us. It would seem that such caution deserves the verdict: where there is no persecution, there can be no freedom, no joy, no Israel of God, and no new creation. Galatians 6:14 is still far too radical for the churches of the U.S.A., as presumably it was for many members of the church in Galatia.

> The dominant picture of God in western orthodoxy, whether Roman or Protestant, has been as the foremost advocate of law and order. . . . A religion of law and order is the cult of Caesar; when it is carried into the church it becomes the tyranny of the AntiChrist.[18]

If this be true, it follows that the message of the resurrection cannot really be heard by such a church, for that message presupposes the triple crucifixion. Paul's ability to glory only in Christ's cross is his own prophetic witness to the hard fact of resurrection. This contrast between Paul and our American churches becomes the more apparent when we ask where people usually locate evidence to support the Christian confession "he arose from the dead." For many Christians, whether scholars, ministers, or laymen, the most convincing evidence is provided by the report of an empty tomb.

> The empty tomb stands as the massive sign that the eschatological deed of God is not outside this world of time and space, or in despair of it, but has laid hold of it, penetrated deep into it, shattered it, and begun its transformation.[19]

For Paul (not only in Gal. 6:15, but in many other texts, such as 1 Cor. 15; Phil. 2; Rom. 8) the massive sign of this shattering "deed of God" was quite different; it was the believers' victory over the "*stoicheia* of the world," along with the freedom and persecution bestowed on all who shared in that victory. Without this evidence, faith in the resurrection would have been little more than superstition; with this evidence in hand, the announcement of a new creation became as irrepressible as the joy that accompanies liberation from the most desperate bondage.

To summarize this exploration of Galatians 6:14 let us return to the shorthand terms used in our thought experiment. The perfect passive verbs testify to the decisive identification of the X-event with the cross and resurrection of Christ. The carefully articulated triple crucifixion testifies to the all-inclusive range of the change accomplished there. This event marked the beginning of the new creation which carried with it new horizons for "the Israel of God." It conveyed to Paul a vocation under God which was vindicated by the realities of freedom and persecution, empowered by the gifts of mercy and peace, and oriented toward the hope that belonged to this calling. His Galatian readers had accepted that calling without comprehending the full impact of that calling on their world. The *cosmic* changes that took place in that event are well described in the words of Gabriel Fackre:

The Dark Work of God is the death of the powers that harass us. The swaggering Principalities that seem to control the future have themselves had their future taken away. The social, economic, and political monoliths [Galatians 4 stresses the religious monolith] that dominate our horizon and tyrannize over those struggling for liberation and reconciliation are dust and ashes.... [On the cross] the powers of evil ... received a mortal wound.[20]

Fackre's words summarize what was meant by the world being crucified to the believer; St. Tykhon's words summarize the parallel crucifixion of the believer to the world:

The Son of God humbled himself for you—could you be proud? The Son of God took the form of a servant—could you seek to rule? He became poor—could you run after riches? He accepted dishonor—could you strive after honors?[21]

Before proceeding further with the study, readers are urged to read again in the previous chapter the fourteen theses by which we described "the panorama of that world which comes into view" through the witness to the death-resurrection of Jesus. It can now be asserted that each of those theses is supported and illustrated by the thought of Paul in Galatians. Accordingly we conclude that faith in the resurrection of Jesus is quite impossible apart from active participation in the triple crucifixion by which the new creation is inaugurated, that is, if we follow Galatians 6:14–15. This conclusion encourages us, in turn, to find in these verses a basic resolution of the four problematic areas that were isolated in the initial thought experiment (pp. 36–39).

4
The Vocation to Invisible Powers
Ephesians 3:8–10

*If this (apocalyptic) symbolism should disappear
from the missionary consciousness of the church,
the church would lose its power to combat the
demonries of the present, to confront the agencies
of the counter-Christ with the exorcizing function
of the gospel.* [1]

An understanding of the apostolic vocation of the church is a
necessary step toward understanding the entire complex to
which we have given the alphabetical symbol XYZ. The boundaries of this vocation are marked by a distinctive memory (X)
and an equally distinctive hope (Z). Thus we can designate the
entire course of the apostolic vocation by the letter Y, keeping
in mind, of course, the limitations of such abstract definitions.

There is no need to repeat here what was said about our use
of the term *vocation.* Christian vocation comprises a calling and
a sending by the living Christ whose presence is manifested
both in inner compulsions and in outer tasks. Such a vocation
has the power to redefine the meaning of life for each disciple,
inasmuch as death and rebirth separate the new person from
the old. Moreover, since this same decisive event separates the
children of Sara from the children of Hagar, the "Israel of
God" from the "present Jerusalem" (to use the idiom of Galatians), a close interaction emerges between the communal vocation and the individual vocation. There is only one calling

and only one hope that motivates that calling. According to Ephesians 4:1–16, this communal vocation provides the vantage point from which one can comprehend virtually every basic Christian conviction—about God, the Lord, the Spirit, the body, faith, baptism, grace, peace, meekness, love. Every Christian is under total obligation to "lead a life worthy of this calling" (4:1) and in so doing to recognize the diversity of gifts (4:11). Vocation is a communal movement from Christ's coming to Christ's coming, from X to Z. "Mission, therefore, means to recognize what the Creator-Redeemer is doing in his world, and try to do it with him."[2] In no document is this matter of vocation more central than in Ephesians.

Hostility and Unity

All these assertions, however, are so theoretical, so pontifical, as to glaze the eyes and anesthetize the mind. To escape the coma produced by platitudes we need to ask why this author so strongly stressed the strategic importance of this one calling. The answer almost immediately dispels the smog by introducing us into the arena of a bitter and bruising hostility. This author was dealing with the ancient animosity between Jew and Gentile. Culturally, of course, this conflict antedated the rise of the new faith, and that rise has tended, over the centuries, to accentuate the conflict. So deeply imbedded was this conflict, in fact, that no person who became a follower of Jesus the Messiah could forget or ignore his own earlier identity or that of his fellows, as either Jew or Gentile. I need not argue the point that the inclusion of Gentiles within a community that was initially Jewish signified the awesome power of the gospel. Nor need I stress the point that it has been extremely difficult for later generations of Christians to recall or to repeat the full dimensions of that initial achievement.

Even the author of Ephesians (whom I will call Paul without arguing the question of authorship),[3] though writing to Gentile Christians, gives vivid if unwitting testimony to the strength of current Jewish antipathies. Though we cannot doubt his devotion to the Gentile mission, he spoke of Gentiles as those who had been "far off," as "the uncircumcized," "strangers to the covenants of promise," without God and therefore without hope (2:11ff.). They had been "dead," helpless captives of "the prince of the power of the air" (2:1f.). Their minds had been futile and dark, "greedy to practice every kind of uncleanness" (4:17–19). In short, they had formed one of the only two segments of humanity, whose enmity formed a wall of hostility as thick and strong as "the law of commandments and ordinances" (2:14f.). There could be no clearer expression of dominant Jewish prejudices toward Gentiles, an anti-Gentilism that survived even after Gentile Christians entered the church.

What, then, were the attitudes of Gentiles toward Jews, whether before or after conversion? Some scholars seek to minimize the degree of anti-Semitism, and some to maximize it; and one may suspect that both tendencies are affected by modern debates. Yet, as Douglas Hare points out, "It is perfectly obvious that anti-Semitism did exist in the ancient world prior to and apart from the early church."[4] Moreover, Hare agrees with major conclusions of J. N. Sevenster[5] that the fundamental causes can be traced to Israel's "sovereign self-sufficiency," its "unbounded arrogance," its stubborn refusal to seek assimilation with the dominant culture, and the peculiarities of its religious practices, so foreign and so ridiculous in Gentile eyes.[6] We must assume that some of these attitudes accompanied Gentiles into the church, and that some Gentile Christians would have resisted even more vehemently than Paul the demands of Judaizers. The apostle's curses, so scathing in Galatians against both Judaizers and their Gentile puppets (1:8; 3:10ff.; 5:2–4), must have been mild in comparison with the epithets of some Gentile believers. Nor can we doubt the presence of provocation for these curses, since it is perfectly clear that both Paul and his Gentile converts were subjected to brutal violence not only from unbelieving Jews but even from Jewish Christians (cf. 2 Cor. 11:22–28). The author of Ephesians claims to be in prison because of his stewardship of God's grace for Gentiles, and it is likely that his stigmata (Gal. 6:17) were the wounds from persecution for which Jewish Christians were at least partly responsible. Since Ephesians represents such a conflict, we must grant that any genuine oneness in vocation must have marked an almost miraculous transformation of both Jews and Gentiles.

When we read Ephesians 4 we must give full weight to such a miracle. Not only does the chapter celebrate an unprecedented unity among the first readers; it also is doubtful whether modern Christian readers have experienced anything comparable. We can hardly use that chapter as a description of twentieth-century Christianity without crossing our fingers, or stifling a hoot of derision, or angrily challenging the hypocrisy in any church that piously parrots those liturgical phrases: "you were called to the one hope that belongs to your calling" (4:4).

This calling carries with it the implicit archaeology, teleology, and eschatology which the author of Ephesians made explicit.[7] Archaeology: They had been called in Christ before the foundation of the world (1:4). Teleology: They had a part in the continuing growth of the "whole structure . . . into a holy temple in the Lord" (2:21). Eschatology: God's plan is "to unite all things in him, things in heaven and things on earth" (1:10). Wherever the gifts of grace appeared, there could be discerned the inner compulsions and the outer impact of this one vocation (4:7). All their behavior was to be measured and motivated by a life worthy of this calling (4:1). In fact, we must not ignore the fact that participation in this one vocation provides the necessary hermeneutical premise for the other "onenesses" of the text: the body, the Spirit, faith, baptism, the Lord, the Father. It was that vocation into which the Gentile readers of Ephesians had been inducted, and it was that very induction that had incited civil war among the followers of Jesus Christ.

One index to this ancient situation is provided by the use of pronouns in this Epistle. Normally the second person is used to address the Gentiles who have become faithful saints (1:1). (In many places this reference of the pronoun is unmistakable:

2:1, 2, 8, 11–13; 3:1–6; 4:17–5:20. We are therefore justified in assuming the same intention in other texts: 1:2, 13, 15–18; 2:16–19; 4:1–6; 5:21–6:24.) Ephesians is different from other Paulines in that it appears to be addressed solely to Gentiles. As we have noted, the author speaks of their preconversion status in a most negative way; he also deplores their tendency to continue within the church their unconverted patterns of behavior (4:17ff.). So much for the second person.

When the author speaks of himself as *I*, he normally distinguishes himself from the uncircumcized readers. He is a representative of the commonwealth of Israel as well as a missioner of Jesus. He is bound to these readers only by this vocation as a prisoner on their behalf and as a steward of God's grace for them (1:15f.; 3:1f., 7–14; 4:1, 17; 6:19–22).

His practice is strikingly different when he uses the first person plural. Now he is influenced, by the oneness of their calling, to include the Gentile readers with himself. Hardly ever, if ever, does he use *we*, *us*, or *our* to distinguish Jewish believers from Gentile believers. *A* typical change may be noted in the transition from 1:2 to 1:3, where "Grace to *you*" becomes "Blessed be God who has blessed *us*." This quiet change in pronouns signals the destruction of the highest wall in the ancient world, highest at least when measured by his Jewish brothers. (For other instances of the change from *you* to *us*, see 1:14; 2:3, 10, 14–18; 3:20, 21; 4:6, 13–16; 5:2, 30; 6:12.)

An even more decisive signal is provided by his use of the words *all* and *one*. We are usually too drugged by the inflation of pious rhetoric, when Scripture is being read, to detect the echoes of revolution which those tiny words celebrate. Both are used in Ephesians to mark the miraculous inclusion of Gentiles and Jews in the one body, the same new humanity, a single temple. At virtually every occurrence of these words, the reader should pause to ponder the majestic cosmic scope of that miracle. In that pondering, we should recall the anti-Gentile attitudes as voiced by Paul himself, the probable anti-Semitic reactions among Gentile believers, and the violence of the civil war among other Christian communes, as in Galatia or Philippi. The force of those pronouns and numerals should be kept in mind as we turn to the analysis of the triple definition of vocation in 3:8–10.

The One Vocation

To me, though I am the very least of all the saints, this grace was given, [1] to preach to the Gentiles the unsearchable riches of Christ, [2] to make all men see what is the plan of the mystery hidden for ages in God who created all things, [3] that through the church the manifold wisdom of God might now be made known to the principalities and powers in the heavenly places.

In all three clauses the emphasis falls upon the communication of knowledge, though knowledge of a rare sort. As a prophet the apostle has been charged with revealing heavenly secrets. This wisdom conveys unsearchable riches and discloses a primordial divine plan for all things. The prophet has seen and has been commissioned to tell his readers what he has seen.[8] We may note a progression in the identity of the revealers of this wisdom: in the first two instances the revealer is the apostle himself; in the third, the revealer is the church.

There is also a significant progression in the identity of the audiences. Each of the three audiences merits separate attention. First is the audience of Gentiles for whom Paul had received a special mandate. His self-denigration ("least of all the saints") recalls his earlier opposition to the gospel, and especially to the Gentile mission, an opposition that had made all the more remarkable God's choice of him for that very mission. Here, however, that calling is seen to be a step toward a wider audience: "all men." That is the current RSV translation which will surely be changed in the next edition. For "all men" is the translation for *pantas,* and that translation is now seen by many readers to imply a masculinity not present in the Greek text. Even the word *pantas* (all) is missing from some Greek manuscripts, though a majority of manuscripts and of commentators favor its retention.[9] The almost certain reference is to the whole of humanity, corresponding to the "all things" in the same verse. And in the Ephesians context, I am convinced that Paul had in mind the union of Jews and Gentiles within this totality (cf. 2:11–3:6). So the mission of the apostle was oriented toward this double audience: first the Gentiles, and then "the one humanity" to which Jews and Gentiles belonged.

The third audience, like the third messenger, is quite different. The church is charged with making known God's wisdom to principalities and powers in the heavenly places. We must therefore ask further concerning this audience, the nature of the message, and the qualifications of the church to deliver it. For these powers Ephesians has a variety of terms: rulers, lordships, dominions, authorities, names, principalities. We may safely draw inferences concerning their status and work from various statements in Ephesians. They now operate according to a wisdom that is set over against the wisdom of God, of which presumably they have been ignorant (3:10). Although they may be located in heavenly places, their work may be observed in the sons of disobedience, those who live by the passions of the flesh and are dead through their sinful behavior (2:1–3). Their earthly sons as "children of wrath" betray the character of their parents (2:3). Those parents are the ultimate source of all the earthly forces that have carried on the rebellion against God, most clearly disclosed in the enmity that brought Jesus to his death.[10] They have the power to name the various human communities or families and to demand the loyalty of those whom they name. Ephesians identifies a major expression of this power: the building, support, and extension of the walls of division between races, cultures, and religions. Here a very particular wall, for it is these principalities that have made Jews and Gentiles enemies through "the law of commandments and ordinances" (2:14f.) and have prolonged that enmity with their requirement of circumcision. If one wishes to detect their invisible activity, one should examine this dividing wall of hostility, which is nowhere made more visible than in the cross of Christ. This is why his ascension far above these rulers signaled the permanent destruction of all these walls (1:21; 4:8–10).

Modern Christians are frequently baffled by scriptural references to the activities of these powers. This is rather strange in that these same people seem able, without similar bafflement, to affirm faith in the Risen Christ as their lord and savior. Yet this lord is himself an invisible power, exercizing sovereignty from a seat "in the heavenly places" (1:20). The other invisible heavenly powers are denizens of that same realm. It is curious that one set of powers should be more intelligible and credible than the opposing set. Certainly the apostle discerned ample evidence for that continuing warfare, since the powers are responsible for his own imprisonment and for insidious attacks upon the cohesion of the Christian family. That family can win the war with these powers, but only by relying on "the whole armor of God" (6:10–18), weapons especially designed to repel the malice, deceit, and slander which would again break up this family into its former hostile segments. We should not confuse these powers with the forces of secularism, atheism, or irreligion. No, in this case they govern their satellite communities by using religious traditions, laws, sacraments, and loyalties to buttress societal divisions. Any attack on those divisions is a challenge to their hegemony; the emergence of a new community drawn from people on both sides of former barricades marks their demise.

If this is the audience of the church's proclamation, this also indicates the thrust of that message. Our text tells us that it is "the manifold wisdom of God." It stresses two facts about this wisdom: it has been hidden from the ethnic and religious families which those powers have claimed and named (cf. 1 Cor. 2:6–8); it has now been revealed, at least to the church. The hiddenness corresponds to the existence of the walls; the revelation corresponds to their destruction. The wisdom of God is *primal* in that it has always been present in the purpose of the Creator of all things; it is *final* in that the victory of Christ opens an immediate access to God, the God for whom *every* family is named. This access is claimed in faith and is reflected in the boldness and freedom of captives released from former indentures. Their sufferings should not cause depression or doubt, since this wisdom is hidden in the processes by which intercessory activity yields a miraculous increment of glory (3:13). Free men who have been enlisted from both sides of a barricade discover what it is like to live in a community that is rooted and grounded in love; in fact, one might infer that only such freedmen can apprehend the mystery of this love. It is they (and only they?) who are filled with the very fullness of this God (3:14–21).

This is to say that this wisdom and this love are coextensive (3:19); yet there are other things to be said about this wisdom. It is a plan, a design intended to bring about the fullness of time, the unity of all things in Christ. On earth this means the reconciliation of Jews and Gentiles by the destruction of the dividing wall. In heaven there is a corresponding reconciliation of all things through the exaltation of Christ above all competing powers. The development of this plan may be detected by the exercise of this sovereignty over his body by this Head. It is God's intention to create in Christ a community as inclusive as the whole of creation. The gospel story discloses the triumph of that intention, although the disclosure appears to be nullified by continued hostility between Jews and Gentiles. In the midst of such enmity, the gospel can be affirmed by a Jew or a Gentile only on the basis of divine revelation and only by accepting Christ's calling into this new community. Yet when Paul examines the fabric of communal living within the church, he appears to trace every hostile impulse, every claim to superiority, every self-serving religious custom, every invidious rationalization, to the instigation of these heavenly powers. This means that the proclamation of God's wisdom to them can take place only through successive communal victories over such impulses and claims. It is by way of such victories that he visualizes the whole body being joined and knit together.

The character of the message thus dictates the character of the messenger. Since the struggle between God and the no-gods is conceived in these terms, only a community can convey this particular message. Whenever Jews and Gentiles live together in peace, they inform the powers which guard "the law of commandments and ordinances" that their authority has been supplanted by the "law of Christ" (Gal. 5:13–15). They have been crucified with Christ. But only a community can deliver that message, speaking in a language that these powers can understand, the language of actual communal unity. That this language gets through to them is proved by the ferocity and subtlety of their backlash. They do everything they can to disrupt the morale of that community, especially by deceitful appeals to "the good." Accordingly the church can proclaim its message only by meeting this new threat to its cohesion. In Ephesians we can discern three stages in the delivery of this message:

1. The initial formation of the church as a fellowship among erstwhile enemies, which constituted an announcement to the principalities that the dividing wall had been breached.
2. The successful resistance to the backlash from these powers, which constituted continuing evidence that the exalted Christ has taken them captive.
3. The internal growth of the new community into the measure of the stature of the fullness of Christ; this constituted the announcement of the coming destruction of all other dividing walls between nations, races, classes, sexes.

Of all New Testament writings, Ephesians most clearly presents this work as the essential vocation of the church. That is why its images of the unity of the church take such a commanding position. Each of these images is expressive of the archaeology, the teleology, and the eschatology embodied in those three stages: one temple under construction, one body being knit together, one baptism, one new humanity, one warfare with one set of weapons. In this context one should speak not so much of "the unity of the church" as of "the church of the unity," since it is only where this unity in vocation is being realized that the church emerges and grows. This vocation is not a new duty that is now added to a pre-existing entity; rather it is the work through which this new community comes into existence. This is something that no apostle can accomplish; this wisdom is of a kind that no verbal pronouncement can convey. The only language that the heavenly powers can grasp is the language of centripetal communal forces that prove to be strong enough to defeat their centrifugal strategies. This is not to say that the individual prophet or apostle has lost his mandate; his work is simply designed to produce such a community. This observation leads us back to the double indication of Paul's calling in 3:8–9.

First of all, Paul had been summoned as an apostolic prophet to reveal to Gentiles the unsearchable riches of Christ. It was strategic that this work should be done by a Jew sent by a Jewish Messiah to pagan Gentiles. It was doubly strategic that this Jewish emissary should first have been a persecutor of Jewish prophets who had broken through the dividing wall of hostility. It was triply strategic that as a price of his new calling he should himself pay the penalty for breaching that wall: "a prisoner for Christ Jesus on behalf of you Gentiles" (3:1). Strategic, yes. But this was not a strategy designed by Paul; he saw his role as an essential part of God's design, made known to him by revelation (3:3). This strategy had been vindicated by Paul's success in preaching the gospel to Gentiles, when they became "fellow heirs, members of the same body, and partakers of the promise in Christ Jesus" (3:6). Whatever else the apostle may have meant by the unsearchable riches, he clearly meant to say that this Gentile inheritance was in no respect inferior to that of the Jews. It included "every spiritual blessing in the heavenly places," a common origin and a common destiny as elect sons of God (1:3–5). He also meant to say that apart from Christ Jews were heirs of death, along with the rest of mankind (2:3). As in Romans 11:32 Paul proclaimed the death of all apart from Christ and the gift of life to all through Christ. The ultimate wall demolished by

Christ had been the wall between death and life (cf. Rom. 8:35–39); the destruction of the wall between Jew and Gentile was sign of that ultimate earthquake. Surely such riches are rightly termed unsearchable. Not only do these riches free Gentiles from such walls through their obedience to the invisible heavenly power of Christ who has won the victory over all other invisible powers; not only do they confer on Gentiles awesome spiritual blessings "in the heavenly places"; they are the sign that God has "made us sit with him *in the heavenly places*" (2:6). There is every reason, then, why Gentiles who have become "citizens of heaven" should be able to understand the invisible activities of both Christ and his enemies.

Yet God had called Paul to do something more than convert Gentiles. Unless a second task were accomplished, that conversion would simply reinforce the dividing wall and prove the continued power of its heavenly sponsors. He was called to make all Jewish and all Gentile Christians understand the plan of the mystery which had been hidden for ages. Each group of believers had its own set of temptations. For example, Gentile converts might react to Jewish insistence on circumcision by claiming that uncircumcision was even more important. But that would simply have aggravated the hostility. Only when circumcision and uncircumcision had ceased to count for anything would the new creation emerge (Gal. 6:15). Gentile converts must be induced to realize that God's plan required not hostility toward the Jews but peace with them within the same family, in a race-blind, nation-blind, religion-blind community. In this regard Paul's own acceptance of persecution by his Jewish brothers became a touchstone of this double mission. And his mission would fail, unless Gentiles manifested love for the Jews in the one body. But the Jewish Christians also had their special temptations which could only be overcome if they fully understood God's plan. They must welcome without reservation the creation of one new man to replace the two. They must be made jealous (Rom. 11:13–16). They must have their deepest convictions concerning the uncircumcized Gentiles reversed as Paul's had been. When that had happened, and only then, could the church be in a position to preach the gospel to the principalities and powers. Paul therefore had a mission to Jewish as well as to Gentile converts; both groups must understand the mystery of reconciliation to one another through the "one body."

It should now become clear how the various vocations were integrated: the vocation of Paul, the prophetic revealer of God's plan; the vocation of every member of this one body, whether Jew or Gentile; the vocation of the new community to disclose Christ's victory over the heavenly powers. No one who had been "made alive together with Christ" could escape a share in that vocation, in its one hope of attaining "mature manhood" (4:13). Gordon Rupp has described this one vocation in vivid terms:

> That community becomes a kind of Lidice, Buchenwald, Leningrad in reverse, in which revenge and hatred have been swallowed up in love and reconciliation.[11]

This vocation cannot be separated from Paul's vision of all things; in fact this vocation *is* his theology. One can locate authentic Pauline theology only where this vocation is being continued, with all its costs and its successes.

Paradigmatic Relevance

Having completed the exegetical task, we now ask what perennial significance this analysis of the one vocation may have. Any answer that is cogent must reckon with the vast changes in situation between then and now. We cannot assume that the division of human society into Jew and Gentile remains the prime factor in the Christian mission. Before seeking to answer the question of relevance we must abstract from the ancient situation some pattern of convictions that was intrinsic to that situation and that remains applicable today. Such a pattern can be constructed, with some ten features remaining constant. These are:

— The division of human society into at least two hostile segments.

— The claim by one segment that its hostility to the other is required by its obedience to God's will, and that its superiority stems from its role as God's elect.

— The commission of an able representative of that community to go to the enemy community with an assurance of God's election and grace that denies any claim to superiority and undercuts any reason for continued separation of the two segments.

— The acceptance of this commission by this representative, and his consequent persecution by both ancestral communities.

— Through his work the emergence of a new community composed of members from both sides of the dividing wall, signifying its obsolescence.

— The conviction of this new community that its existence represents both the initial purpose of the Creator of all things and an initial stage in his final unification of all things.

— The mounting of violent attacks by both ancestral communities on this new community, attacks which raise serious doubts about its power to survive.

— The discovery by this new community of inner resources for resisting these attacks and for using the emergency to strengthen the bonds of mutual dependence.

— Its readiness to substitute for the normal self-defense of communal rights the practice of intercessory suffering, so that its freedom and joy may be extended to others who are still captive to communal self-interest.

— The manifest intention to move forward from the demolition of one wall of division to the destruction of all similar walls within society: racial, economic, national, sexual, religious.

Let us now assume these ten features as a rough profile of a paradigm and inquire where we may locate in our world today an activity that is analogous. This is serious business, indeed, if we use the presence of this paradigm as a decisive criterion for locating the life of the new temple, the new man, the body of Christ. Using this criterion we may be forced to admit the virtual abdication by our churches of all three aspects of that vocation which is described in Ephesians 3:8–10. Consider the churches in Lebanon, Angola, Rhodesia, Northern Ireland, South Korea, or typical congregations and denominations in the U.S.A. Are they able to comprehend, not to say accept or pursue, this triple vocation? When we and our people worship before an altar on which a cross stands, do we discern in that cross an eternal victory over all the invisible powers that divide humanity into warring factions, a victory which we can celebrate only by meeting reconciled enemies at that same altar, a victory that impels us to proclaim peace to principalities and powers by seeking the most acute battle line and standing there as witness to Christ's death? Where is the bishop who serves as successor to this apostle? Where the seminary that trains neophytes in this triple task? Where the missionary society whose program and support are geared to produce a community like this? No hermeneutical trick can diminish the distance between the Ephesians paradigm and the sense of vocation among contemporary churches. Into that vacuum have rushed other conceptions of the mission, more closely aligned to the position of Paul's Jewish enemies who "compassed sea and land to make one proselyte" (Matt. 23:-15). It is hard to gainsay the verdict of John V. Taylor:

> Once Christians had begun to think of the church as a structure to be compared to . . . other structures in society, it became one of the very principalities and powers that the gospel was supposed to withstand. So began a long struggle for recognition, privilege and ultimately control. . . . Unable to lose its life in order to save it, the community of the New Man seems willy-nilly to have become . . . just one more of the establishments which are innately predisposed to crucify any new man.[12]

Where this counterrevolution has succeeded, where the Ephesians paradigm has been long repudiated, what else happens? One thing is sure. Where dividing walls are no longer being demolished, churches will never reckon the defeat-victory of Jesus to be the most important recent event in history. Rather will they join the scoffers of 2 Peter for whom "all things have continued as they were from the beginning of creation" (3:4). Such churches will provide sad evidence for the failure of Paul's mission. Refusing to share in a similar mission they will avoid the persecution accorded to genuine disciples and forfeit the joys of sharing the unsearchable riches with former enemies. They will stand as signs of the power of the "prince of the air," signs of the failure of God's plan for the unification of all things.

In such churches there will of course remain various causes of division, but how serious will they be? Consider, for example, the internal struggle between proponents of individual evangelism and proponents of social reform. Does either of these groups show full respect for the apostolic authority and example of Paul? In comparison with a third alternative—the mission to principalities and powers—will either of these alternatives disclose any profound grasp of the forces that accomplished the death of Jesus, or the enemies against whom the church should continue to fight? If neither can produce a community in which archetypal hostilities have been overcome by the cross, neither can proclaim the primordial plan of God to the rulers of this darkness.

Or one may reflect upon the division between advocates of dialogue with other religions and their opponents for whom such dialogue would betray the uniqueness of Christianity. Can the church claim to understand the manifold wisdom of God when it is unable to resolve the hostility between these two types of strategy? Can a community that has defected on the Pauline vocation be trusted to recognize or to defend the "uniqueness" of the gospel? Where does that uniqueness appear if not in the paradigm that destroys every dividing wall? Does that paradigm require dialogue with enemies or abstention from that dialogue? Can we ever penetrate the hiddenness of God's method of reconciliation until we discover within ourselves (it may be in our anti-Semitism) awful correspondences to the anti-Gentilism of the Israel of Paul's day? According to Paul, the only entry into the new creation comes through the recognition that neither circumcision nor uncircumcision counts for anything (Gal. 6:14–15). Can or does any of our churches now say *that* with regard to its own "law of commandments and ordinances"?

It has become popular for Christians to speak of the church as "the sign of the coming unity of mankind." But such a sign is hollow unless this unity has coped with the thickest wall of division in our world. Judging by the report of the Fifth Assembly of the World Council of Churches (Report of Section II), the churches prefer to think of unity as comprising "desirable diversity" and pluralism of structures. Such unity, such catholicity, become platitudes that soothe the complacent; they have a very tenuous connection to the peace and love concerning which Paul wrote to the Ephesians. In the gospels the story of the crucifixion and resurrection includes the account of an earthquake (Matt. 27:51–53; 28:2). Paul's vocation to Jews and Gentiles was postearthquake, as was his definition of the mission of the church. By contrast, even the best current definition of the vocation of the churches is preearthquake, and the sign of this is the extent to which the initial wall of hostility has been replaced by quite trivial problems of pluralism and diversity. To call our polite efforts at courtesy signs of the coming unity of mankind is to betray the massive scope of the new creation and the vocation of those who enter it.

Participation in that new creation, the plan of the mystery hidden for ages, is the source of the triple vocation described by Paul. It is small wonder that lack of such participation should produce endless confusion concerning the mission of the church. Small wonder that churches should become demoralized, akin not only to pre-Christian Israel but even more to pre-Christian Gentilism, "without God and without hope in the world." We live and work as if the principalities and powers which erect the dividing walls were in firm control of history. By contrast, Paul could write from prison as if, of all possible situations, the position of the church in the world was a sign of the reconciliation of all enmities. He lived and died in the confidence that all demonic powers had actually been dethroned, and so there radiated from his prison cell a freedom and joy for which we vainly hunger. The verses in Ephesians make quite clear what must happen before any community today can join Paul in his triple vocation.

5
The Bridge Between Generations
John 17:20–24

*The preaching of the Christian gospel was
always and everywhere scandalous and offensive.* [1a]

*No thinking person can still believe that a personal
God, in order to redeem mankind, sent his personal son
to be incarnate, and to be executed, on this earth, and
then made him rise from the dead. We have to listen to
the voice of reason about that kind of myth and symbolism.* [1b]

We have traced in Ephesians the profile and impetus of the
church's proclamation to heavenly powers. That notion of the
church's task is only one of many such notions to be located
within the New Testament.[2] To balance the picture we should
look at a presentation of the church's message to the world
which is found in the Gospel of John. A fascinating formula-
tion of this vocation is expressed in the prayer of Jesus in
chapter 17.

The Two Generations
In literary terms, this chapter forms a major turning point in
the narrative; attention here shifts from Jesus' "love for his
own" to the hour when he would "depart out of this world to
the Father" (13:1). The quiet interlude of conversation with
"his own" is soon to be broken by the noisy arrest and tumul-

tuous trial. The prayer forms a highly dramatic preface to the Passion, "Father, the hour has come; glorify your son," but it also serves as a poignant coda to those same events, "I glorified you on earth, having accomplished the work which you gave me to do" (17:1ff.). In liturgical use, the prayer became an essential link between the events of the Passion and the later Eucharistic celebration of those events. As the longest prayer ascribed to Jesus anywhere in the Bible, it articulates a complex and subtle fabric of attitudes toward the Father, the disciples, and the world. To Jewish Christian readers, it called to mind the equally symbolic farewell address of Moses to the twelve tribes (Deut. 29–33). Just as Jesus was viewed as a prophet-king like Moses, so his band of disciples was viewed as reminiscent of the twelve tribes. As Moses' farewell and final charge took the form of an extended blessing on Israel, so Jesus interceded for his followers, praying for the success of their work.[3] Because of their strategic location and significance, then, we should treat the thrust of Jesus' petitions with utmost seriousness.

The prayer consists of three paragraphs. First comes an accounting with the Father that covers Jesus' entire assignment "to give eternal life to all whom you have given him" (vv. 1–5). Then comes a plea for those disciples with whom he was then standing, those for whom he had "consecrated" himself during the preceding weeks (vv. 6–19). Finally another group comes into view when he intercedes for "those who believe in me through their word" (vv. 20–26). This third paragraph appears to be the center of gravity for the prayer as a whole. These last two paragraphs mention two distinct groups of followers whom we may call disciples at first hand and disciples at second hand, those who followed Jesus before his glorification and those who later accept the testimony *(logos)* of the first group. The wording of the prayer implies that this distinction was important, and that it had been bridged by Jesus' love for both groups.

We therefore conclude that something of a generation gap existed, at least in the evangelist's own church, although we can only conjecture the emotional components of this gap. In some respects the disciples at first hand may have felt superior or advantaged, the disciples at second hand inferior and disadvantaged. This would not be surprising, since in the early church great weight attached to those who had known Jesus directly. For us who live many generations later, the distance between the first and the second generation has shrunk in significance. It is difficult to recover the initial situation. But it may help if we recall that a high risk attended discipleship in those days. Social ridicule, ostracism, hatred, a martyr's death—these were not only the possible but the common fate of disciples. This risk would itself serve to distinguish those who had been called by Jesus himself from those who were wagering such high stakes on the reliability of later testimonies to Jesus. However we explain the distance between the two generations, Jesus is portrayed in his prayer as vitally concerned "that they all may be one," that is, that the two generations should become more united. The prayer intimates that an essential feature of Jesus' vocation was the building of this bridge between the generations. The prayer also clarifies the conviction that this unity would have a value for their mission: "that the world may know that you have sent me." Later we will examine the connections between this unity and this knowledge; now we review other passages in the Gospel where these two generations are distinguished in order that their separation may be overcome.

We may look first at the three visions of the ascended Lord in chapters 20 and 21, in all three of which the Lord shows a strong concern for the disciples at second hand. In the first vision they come into view as the men and women whose sins will be forgiven by the eleven disciples after they have received the Holy Spirit and have been sent out by the glorified Lord (20:23). In the second vision they appear as recipients of the beatitude: "blessed are those who have not seen and yet believe" (20:29). Readers easily overlook the fact that this beatitude is the intended climax of the encounter between Jesus and Thomas, but the fact is undeniable. To be sure, Jesus took care of Thomas's hesitations, but he was even more careful of the situation of those believers who would not have the benefit of seeing the signs recorded in the Gospel, including that very vision of the Risen Lord. So he turns Thomas's attention away from his own predicament toward the needs of those to whom Thomas and the others would be sent.

Parenthetically, we observe that the evangelist in the very next sentence indicates a desire that his own written account may serve as one substitute for the advantages of the disciples at first hand. By reading this narrative, readers without those privileges may be brought to faith and to a share in eternal life.

In the third vision, the disciples at second hand are given an even more prominent, albeit symbolic, role. They are the fish that at first elude the seven fishermen, until they follow the instructions of their master. When they follow that guidance, the size of their catch amazes them. The fact that there is only one net, and that it remains untorn in spite of the huge catch, is an impressive symbol both of the size and the unity of the church which is to result from their labors. It is even possible that the specified number of fish, 153, corresponds to the total number of species of fish identified by ancient icthyologists; if so, this numeral may symbolize the way in which disciples at second hand will represent all sorts and conditions of humanity.[4]

Another symbol, with similar implications, is provided by the flock of sheep and lambs which Peter is commanded to feed. According to the dialogue between Jesus and this future leader of the church, the key test of his love for the master will be his care for the disciples at second hand, a care which in the end will lead to Peter's martyrdom. Even the role of the beloved disciple becomes significant in terms of the subsequent generation, since his testimony will become the basis for their faith (21:24).

Still another proof of Jesus' concern for this second generation of disciples may be found in the elaborate allegory of the good shepherd, the false shepherds, the under-shepherds, and the flock in chapter 10. The true shepherd gives his life for his flock, while the hireling flees at the first sign of danger. But which groups constitute the flock? The answer must obviously include those disciples in the midst of whom he gave his life. But the answer must also include "other sheep who are not of this fold" (v. 16). When they later heed his voice, they will be brought by the same shepherd into this one flock. Who are they? One might suppose that they are the Gentile Christians who would later become members of the church.[5] Or they might be a deviant theological tradition to be brought back into harmony with a centrist position. But much the simplest hypothesis is to think of these other sheep as those who will believe in Jesus through the word of the first disciples (as in 17:20), those who will believe without having seen (as in 20:-29), and those whom Peter is commissioned to feed (as in 21:15). These sheep would include the first readers of the Gospel, who are here assured that the shepherd laid down his life also for them in keeping with God's assignment (10:18), and that he placed his power at the service of all believers without distinction. To receive him is to have life "abundantly," that is, a life that overflows into the lives of others who come to faith through one's own word (v. 10).

More than any other gospel writer, John gives frequent notice of the continuing chain of witnessing. The earliest disciples came to Jesus through the word of John the Baptizer (1:35–39; 10:41). Peter came through the invitation of Andrew, Nathanael through Philip (1:40–51). Samaritans first believed because of a woman's word (4:39); Mary responded to Martha's declaration, while their brother brought the claims of Jesus to the attention of many Jews (12:10). At crucial points the beloved disciple recognizes the truth before Peter does (21:7), and both of them respond to the message of Mary Magdalene. That same Mary hears the voice of Jesus in the words of a gardener. It is difficult, in fact, to locate in this Gospel any disciple who is not indebted to the testimony of another.

Or consider the allegory of the vine, with its analysis of the functions of vinedresser, vine, branches, and fruit (15:1–17).

The whole allegory focuses upon the productivity of the branches. Only a fruitful branch (a disciple who is instrumental in securing another) can be said to abide in the vine. Such abiding in this vine calls for loving friends by laying down one's life for them. This is the point at which the second generation emerges. But the concern of the vinedresser is not alone the production of fruit; he desires that this fruit should abide (v. 16). Here again the emphasis falls upon Jesus' intention to forge as strong a bond with disciples at second hand as with their predecessors. Those latter-day disciples could therefore be as secure in their faith and as clear in their vocation. The oneness of vine and branches was not a matter that depended on any preferred time or place.

In this Gospel, the bridge between successive generations was further supported by the dispatch of Jesus' *alter ego*, the Counselor or Advocate, who would continue the same work of judging the world and of communicating the truth to it. The second generation might not see the same signs, but wherever this Counselor was present, they would have unimpeded access to both the Father and the Son. Disciples at second hand would never become second class citizens of the kingdom or secondary heirs of Jesus' love or of the joys which that love released.

Similar nuances are present in many passages where John used the words *one* and *all*. The word *one* often carried the implicit negative, *not two; all* similarly implied *not some*. The two words appear together in the prayer, "that they *all* may be *one.* " Another pregnant use of *one* may be found in the unwitting witness of Caiaphas, who

> prophesied that Jesus should die for the nation, and not for the nation only, but to gather into *one* the children of God who are scattered abroad. (11:51f.)

This surely conveys a typical Johannine idea of the vocation of Jesus after his death as well as before it.

The inclusive connotation of *all* appears in many places, but nowhere more succinctly than in the prologue: "to all who believed in his name [including you disciples at second hand] he gave power to become children of God, who were born, not of blood nor of the will of the flesh, nor of the will of men, but of God" (1:12; cf. also 1:16f.; 3:8, 15f.; 6:35–40; 12:46; 18:37). Thus the whole Gospel may be seen as a way of spelling out the prayer "that they all may be one"; a distinction is drawn between two generations, but the ravine between those generations is bridged by their oneness.

The Measure of Oneness

This idea of oneness can, however, become almost wholly devoid of specific content. *One* means *not two,* but in what does this oneness consist? The Johannine text gives an immediate answer: "as you, Father, are in me and I in you, that they may also be in us" (17:21). But for many readers that answer simply conveys nothing but pious fog. How can we penetrate the meanings embodied in this formula? In what respects are this Father and this Son one? How do they abide in one another? Much depends upon finding specific answers to those questions. The immediate context provides several clues, though here again the words often frustrate thought rather than guide it. In view here is a oneness of glory, which is given from God first to Jesus and then to all disciples. That term *glory,* however, may be as baffling in its generality or opaqueness as the term *one.* A second clue is the term *love,* which is seen to move constantly in the same direction, from Father to Son to disciples. Unfortunately, this clue has many possible meanings which do not fit in these particular sentences. Moreover, in popular discourse the word *love* has become so conventional or hackneyed or sentimental that the Johannine intention is distorted. The term *knowledge* provides a third clue. Jesus has made known to one generation the name of God and he will continue to make it known to later generations, so that this same knowledge will bind all into one. Yet for many readers this type of knowledge leaves no sharp or precise imprint on their minds. Still a fourth clue is the idea of sending and being sent. God sends Jesus, who in turn sends his disciples, so that the world may become responsive to the sender through the sent. This one sending, that stretches from God to the world, helps to make the other clues (glory, knowledge, love) more tangible. There is, however, still another Johannine image that makes even more specific the kind of sending that is involved. This is the verb *to work* and the noun *work*. Consider the following assertions:

1. Jesus said to them, "My food is to do the will of him who sent me, and to accomplish his work." (4:34)
2. We must work the works of him who sent me, while it is day. (9:4)
3. The works which the Father has granted me to accomplish, these very works which I am doing, bear me witness that the Father has sent me. (5:36)
4. The Son can do nothing of his own accord, but only what he sees the Father doing; for whatever he does, that the Son does likewise. For the Father loves the Son, and shows him all that he himself is doing; and greater works than these will he show him, that you may marvel. For as the Father raises the dead and gives them life, so also the Son gives life to whom he will. (5:19ff.)
5. The works that I do in my Father's name, they bear witness to me; but you do not believe, because you do not belong to my sheep. My sheep hear my voice, and I know them, and they follow me; and I give them eternal life, and they shall never perish, and no one shall snatch them out of my hand. (10:25ff.)
6. This is the work of God that you believe in him whom he has sent. (6:29)
7. If I am not doing the works of my Father, then do not believe me; but if I do them, even though you do not believe me, believe the works that you may know and understand that the Father is in me and I am in the Father. (10:37ff.)
8. I glorified you on earth, having accomplished the work which you gave me to do. (17:4)

9. The words that I say to you I do not speak on my own
authority; but the Father who dwells in me does his
works. Believe me that I am in the Father and the Father
in me; or else believe me for the sake of the works themselves. Truly, truly I say to you, he who believes in me will
also do the works that I do, and greater works than these
will he do, because I go to the Father. Whatever you ask
in my name I will do it, that the Father may be glorified
in the Son. (14:10ff.)

The common element in all these texts is the idea of vocation. Some of the passages (1 and 2) show a one-to-one correspondence between the works of God and those of Jesus. In
those works the will of God in sending Jesus coincides with the
purpose of Jesus in being sent (1, 2, and 3). In various ways,
the doing of these works becomes a basic constituent of glory
(8 and 9), of love (4), and of knowledge (5 and 7), terms which
we found to be central in the intercessory prayer. We cannot
fail to note how this idea of works helps to define oneness: the
oneness of the Father and the Son consists of their doing the
same works (4). That same principle determines the oneness
of the disciples with both Son and Father (9). In this chain of
workers, the texts stress a steady incremental feature: first the
Son does greater works (4), and then the disciples do greater
works (9), perhaps because the works of the one sent mark the
completion and the vindication of the vocation of both sent
and sender. To believe in a person who has been sent is to
believe in the one who sent him (7). The whole effort of the
one sent is to secure faith in the sender; this faith must take
the form of doing the same works (5, 6, and 7). It is assumed
throughout the Gospel that the author and his readers belong
within the same chain, continuing the sequence of glory,
knowledge, love, and of being sent and doing the same works.
A single process spans the years and the generations of believers.

Since the common accent falls upon the idea of works, we
need to ask for a more exact definition of that idea. Several
texts provide that definition:

the Father raises the dead and gives them life (4)
the Son gives life to whom he will
> I give them eternal life
> they shall never perish
> no one shall snatch them out of my hand (5)

He who believes me . . . greater works than these will he
do (9)
These are written that you may believe and believing may
have life in his name (20:30f.)

This chain of verses gives sharp specificity to the nature of the works: to raise the dead and give them life. It is this that delivers from vagueness and banality such phrases as *in me, in him, in you*. Nothing could demonstrate oneness more strikingly than for the dead to be raised through the work of the disciples, the Son, and the Father. It is this pattern of thinking that clarifies the vocation of Jesus and that discloses the bond between his vocation and that of the disciples, whether at first or second hand. The bond is nothing less than the resurrection of the dead.

This impels us now to ask: *how* are these dead raised? There is one answer in the Gospel and only one. We cannot miss it. Jesus gave life to the dead by laying down his life for them. Only this dying man could raise other dead men to life. How do his disciples give life to the dead? The same answer is inescapable (15:12–17). Now we have glimpsed the underlying pattern of thought:

— the prayer for oneness of the generations
— the measure of oneness: the Father and the Son
— the sharing of glory, love, knowledge, being sent
— the vocation: doing the works
— the character of these works: raising the dead
— the manner of raising the dead: to die for them

We must not pass hastily over this point, because it is the essential key to all other points. Jesus' work is nothing less than to give life to the dead, and that work can only be accomplished by his dying for them. Moreover it is precisely this work of the Son that constitutes the work of the Father. In *this* work they are *one*. This gives at least a double dimension to Jesus' death, a matter which Pascal long ago recognized:

> Jesus suffers in his passion the torments which men inflict upon him, but in his agony he suffers the torments which he inflicts upon himself. . . . This is a suffering from no human but an almighty hand, for he must be almighty to bear it.[6]

It staggers the imagination to contemplate such matters. Even more staggering to carry this understanding further and to apply the oneness of Father and Son to the oneness of believers. To return to the petition of Christ immediately before his Passion, the world will believe in God as the sender of Jesus only if the followers of different generations manifest *this* kind of oneness, and only when this happens will the work of raising the dead be accomplished.

Beginning and End

We return to the final petition in the intercessory prayer of Jesus, which, as we have seen, reflected his concern for the disciples at second hand.

> Father, I desire that they also, whom you have given me, may be with me where I am, to behold my glory which you have given me in your love for me before the foundation of the world. (17:24)

That petition offers to the interpreter an excellent example of what we have called the p/f component in Johannine thought. In the earlier petition we noted that Jesus' vocation included that of creating a oneness on the part of all disciples, and that the vocation of that "one flock" included persuading the world to believe. Now we observe that the primal component in that vocation is traced to a time "before the foundation of the world." Anchored in the very act of creation is God's love for Jesus and his gift of glory to Jesus. This means that, because the mission of the church is continuous with the life-giving work of Jesus, that mission has the same ultimate origin. The participation of disciples in the Son and the Father makes them sharers in glory, life, light, truth; all of these realities are preexistent with God. The effective link between this primal impulse and each successive proclamation of the gospel is seen to be *the word of life,* which was in the beginning with God (1:2). This word bridges every gulf between the generations and enables every believer to relate each day's experience to his call by the Creator of all things.

It is, however, very difficult for modern readers to recapture this sense of primal reality, since that sense collides so directly with our notions of space and time. It is almost impossible for us to trust any "word," however awesome, as having its origins "before the foundation of the world" and as carrying with it the life-giving potencies of the Eternal God. The whole span of time since then seems to cut us off from aboriginal time. Not so for the evangelist. At the outset of his narrative he declares that "the word that was God" has actually chosen to dwell "among us, full of grace and truth." To readers of the second or third generations of faith he could underscore the assurance: "from his fullness have we all received." The reality of incarnation was not limited to an earlier period but became inseparable from the life given through Christ to disciples at second hand.[7]

The Gospel has many ways of describing this link to the Alpha point. The one who came after John was the one who was before John (1:30). He came after Abraham, yet was before Abraham (8:58). Since creation preceded sin, Jesus' primal word could take away the sin of the world. Since light was created before darkness, Jesus as the light could heal human blindness. His "temple" far antedated the temple in Jerusalem, and would therefore outlast it (2:21). His coming as light disclosed the darkness which men had come to love (3:19). On the other hand, those who came to this light disclosed the fact that their works "had been wrought in God," authentic signs of his creative work (3:21). Whoever receives the Son receives the A-life, but disobedience indicates continuing residence in the realm of God's wrath (the C-death). Readers should notice how Jesus defended his cures on the Sabbath: "My Father is working still and I am working" (5:17). Here there is an implicit reference to Genesis 1, to the days of the first week, before God rested on the seventh day. Jesus identified his vocation with the work of God before the first Šabbath. His Jewish antagonists recognized the implication of this riddle, that it made Jesus equal with God (5:18). This primal origin of Jesus' vocation was manifested not only in his cure of sickness and forgiveness of sin but also in his authority over "all who are in the tombs" (5:28), since death had originated as a judgment on sin. When a person believes in Jesus, his word and work become God's word and work (6:28); since God's *logos* now abides in them, they can see and hear the Father whose word and work this is (5:37–42), a word and a work to be identified with the divine act of creation.

We can summarize these various clues to the p component by returning to the farewell prayer of chapter 17. We observe that there are four links between the disciples and the period before the foundation of the world: (1) God's love for Jesus is a primal motivational force; (2) this love conveys a primal glory to its recipients; (3) this love and glory are expressed in God's gift to Jesus of these disciples from successive generations; (4) this chain of life-giving is the continuing chain of self-giving. So much for the Johannine idea of the beginnings of Christian vocation.

The same prayer also articulates a typically Johannine conception of the end, although this conception often eludes the attention of readers. The central purpose of Jesus and the mysterious destiny of disciples are formulated thus: "that they may be with me where I am" (17:24). The discussion of this destiny had formed a continuing thread through the preceding chapters. Jesus had promised that his disciples would go with him where he was going, but he had also warned them that they were not yet ready to go there (13:33, 36). Both promise and warning puzzled them, because they could not yet understand what must first happen. Before their reunion with him could be realized, he must go to prepare a place (his death?), he must come again to them (his ascension?), and they must learn the way to the Father (14:1–7). It was Thomas's mistake to suppose that before they could know the way they must know the goal. The logic of this way and goal was quite the reverse: only those who know the way can discover the goal. The movement toward the Father proceeds by way of doing the works of the Father, by way of life-giving. Along that road to the Father they would learn how the Father and the Son come to disciples to make their home with them (14:23). Jesus' call for them to surrender their lives for love's sake was supported by the promise, "that where I am you may be also" (14:3), and by the amazing assurance, "If you ask anything in my name, I will do it" (14:14). Inasmuch as sharing in the same vocation means sharing in eternal life, those who do Christ's works can be trusted to ask anything in his name. All this, and more, is bound up with Jesus' prayer in 17:24, that his disciples from all generations might be with him "where I am."

We may now point out that John narrates the visions of the risen and glorified Lord in such a way that those visions constitute God's answer to the petition of 17:24. First came the bewilderment and grief of Mary Magdalene over her ignorance of where Jesus had gone. Then came the sharing of that bewilderment by the two disciples, and their scattering to their homes.[8] Then in rapid succession came Mary's vision of the gardener, their mutual recognitions, the announcement of the ascension, and the final set of instructions for his disciples. Then Jesus himself came and stood in their midst with gifts of peace and Spirit, and with his commission. They beheld the glory which God had given to him before the foundation of the world. Because he had come to them, they could be with him where he was, in fishing, in eating breakfast, in feeding his flock, in testifying to the *logos of life,* the word that had become flesh and had taken up its dwelling with them. They had become one, so that the world might believe that God had sent him (17:21). This oneness of mutual indwelling became the Z-point of their vocation; it provided the horizon of their own self-giving.

We can now observe the subtle correspondence between the p component and the f component, which together form a single horizoning. The goal of being "where he is" corresponds to the origin of his primal love and glory. These ultimate horizons are seen to be intimately involved in the doing of the works which form the day's agenda, an agenda that includes love for one another and the mission to the world. The acceptance of that agenda produces a radical alteration in conceptions of space and time, not unlike the alteration described by W. H. Auden:

> *Space is the Whom our loves are needed by,*
> *Time is our choice of How to love and Why.* [9]

Furthermore, the alteration in the community's sense of vocation and avocation is not unlike that intimated by Robert Frost:

> *But yield who will to their separation,*
> *My object in living is to unite*
> *My avocation and my vocation*
> *As my two eyes make one in sight.*
> *Only where love and need are one,*
> *And the work is play for mortal stakes,*
> *Is the deed ever really done*
> *For Heaven and the future's sakes.* [10]

In quoting from Auden and Frost I do not, of course, mean to identify Johannine thought with theirs. Each author has his own distinctive vocabulary and gives to each pivotal term a different cluster of connotations. So, too, there are significant contrasts between Johannine, Pauline, and Marcan idioms. However if one measures their congeniality more by vocation than by vocabulary, the contrasts make the consensus all the more amazing. In John, as we have seen in Paul and will see in Mark, the community's memories focus upon the Passion of Jesus as revealing God's purpose and power. Its hopes point toward a rendezvous with Jesus, where "his own" will abide in him and with him "where he is." During the interim each generation of believers receives life by sharing in the works of the Father and the Son, so that the world may believe. In all three authors, Christ's resurrection initiates and enables the Christian vocation, and this vocation, in turn, becomes the contemporary mode by which the glorified Lord manifests his presence.

6

The Gathering of the Elect

Mark 13:24–27

The chiasmus *seems to be part of Hebrew thought
itself, whether expressed in poetry or in prose.* [1]

*Jesus Christ, whom the two Testaments regard,
the Old as its hope, the New as its model, and
both as their centre.* [2]

In this chapter we shall attempt to cope with another description of the horizons of Christian vocation. This idea of vocation is indicated by the term *elect;* if there were such a verb as
vocation in the English language we would substitute *"the vocationed"* for *the elect.* The former term is preferable in that it
would avoid any association of "the elect" with "the elite." In
either case, this association is ruled out in Mark 13 because the
group in mind is a company of martyrs (v. 12). Of this vocation
the Son of man is identified as the end, and since it is he who
has called them, he is the beginning as well. This is clear in the
climactic paragraph:

> But in those days, after that tribulation, the sun will be dark-
> ened, and the moon will not give its light, and the stars will be
> falling from heaven, and the powers in the heavens will be
> shaken. And then he will send out his angels, and gather his
> elect from the four winds, from the ends of the earth to the ends
> of heaven.

The Difficulties

Like the entire chapter that precedes it, this paragraph bristles with difficulties. Many readers find it virtually impossible to understand a prospect of this sort, let alone accept it. It makes little sense to date an assembly of the saints by a darkened sun and falling stars. Must a believer accept such a prediction? At first glance it would appear that this prediction refers to a single historical event that can be dated on the future time-line, and perhaps scheduled like an appointment with the doctor. We assume that, should such an event take place, the purpose of the prediction would have been exhausted, and its further relevance destroyed, along with last year's datebook. We assume that should this event not in fact transpire, the whole prediction would be invalidated.[3] On the basis of those assumptions, we measure the prediction by our knowledge of the past, and we are forced to conclude (whether gladly or sadly is immaterial) that the prediction is indeed obsolete. Respect for Scripture is diminished accordingly. If we could, even at this late date, delete this chapter from the Holy Book, we would do so. The primary question seems to be this: does our view of the world permit us to take seriously this cluster of expectations? A negative answer seems inevitable.

In dealing with Mark, however, we are obligated to think first of the author and of his initial audience. This should impel us to recognize that they would confront a different set of difficulties. What were they? These people lived before human imaginations were controlled by the mythology of a time-line. Also, they lived before it became the habit to distinguish sharply between events in the human sphere and events in the cosmic sphere. Their linguistic idiom practiced a metaphorical fusing of the objective and subjective components in personal and corporate experience. It seldom occurred to them even to ask if their view of the world permitted them to accept predictions like these. No, they faced quite a different question: does faithfulness to Christ's calling require such extreme self-sacrifice as this chapter specifies? Is this the way in which he wills that disciples should gain lives by losing them (8:35)? Mark seemed to say that this calling and this prospect were so linked that disciples could not accept one without accepting the other. The prediction simply defined the identity of three horizons: the horizon of God's creation, of Christ's work, and of their own vocation. Even this may sound too abstract and too theological for us. For them the difficulties were immediate and ominous: they were set on a path leading to hatred and to death. This fact gave an awesome content to the demand to lose their lives: what would it mean to save them?

There is another respect in which our reading easily distorts Mark's intent. He spoke of the future in terms of three images, not one: the darkened sun, the budding fig tree, and the returning master. When we read his message, our minds tend to become obsessed with the first because of its incredible and stark finality. This is not wholly wrong, for Mark appealed to the darkened sun as an event so unprecedented and unique as to baffle the mind and to arouse the curiosity. But he also described the same prospect as the budding fig tree in spring, an event as normal and inconspicuous as each day's dawn. The conjunction of the two seemingly incompatible images was intentional. Moreover he compared the same prospect to the return of a landowner to his estate, after a brief absence, to take accounting of his staff's faithfulness to instructions. This image brings into play a quite different set of associations: the specific time span within which a specific community fulfills its assigned work. Of Mark's three metaphorical complexes, this third, coming last, reflects the central concern of both author and readers. The apocalyptic scenario, with its traditional symbolism, simply underscores the significance of this vocation, in which the activity of watching (v. 33) consists of slogging away at the assigned tasks (v. 34). The triple description of the "end" is designed to correspond to those tasks. Christ's gathering of the elect is a fitting reversal of their scattering by his foes. The budding fig tree assures every generation of its participation in the unknown day of harvest. The nocturnal return of the master tells every servant that he must give an account for every duty. These are three quite separate images, but central to all three is a promise and a warning given by the Son of man to his own followers. For them the central issue was not a conflict with prior views of the cosmos but the question whether, in view of all the obstacles, they could persevere in trusting his promises.

The foregoing remarks may help us penetrate obscure features in apocalyptic symbolism by using the distinctive Christian vocation as a baseline for interpretation. They do not, however, remove a more basic difficulty: the apparent arrogance of Mark (if not of Jesus) in claiming for this tiny coterie of sectarian Jewish enthusiasts a strategic role in universal history. To state this difficulty mildly, we may say that the fantasy of a darkened sun appears to express a grandiose sense of self-importance on the part of these sectarians. J. Kovesi has spelled out the dimensions of this fantasy.[4] In the first place, this community understands their conception of God's word as a message addressed not simply to them, but to all humanity, living and dead. They discern in this dramatic action of God a universal purpose that transcends all spatial and temporal boundaries. In the second place, this purpose is such as to impel all persons, without exception, to understand themselves as participants in this all-inclusive drama. Even though a person may not so understand himself, the drama is intolerant enough to dictate a prefabricated role for him and his group. Whether they be friends, neutral onlookers or enemies, the drama anticipated their roles and from within its own plot assigns destinies appropriate for each. Finally, the text of the drama, whether oral or written, points beyond itself to the emergence of a community in whose history the drama realizes its own enactment. The text sanctifies this community, and this community in turn sanctifies this text; the megalomaniac claims of the text become the megalomaniac faith of the community; the hopes promised in Scripture encourage the community to project its own communal self-interests upon the vast screen of cosmic history. The cosmic events pictured in Mark 13:24–27 thus represent a colossal expression of this arrogance. Or so it may seem.

Such considerations must not be shunted aside by an interpreter of the Marcan apocalypse. They may well justify the judgment that 13:24–27 is the most problematic paragraph in the most problematic chapter of the Gospel. We cannot, of course, expect to resolve the cluster of riddles posed by that paragraph; we trust, nevertheless, that a consideration of Mark's understanding of vocation may have some value in dealing with those issues. It may be helpful to glance first at some less baffling promises issued to the elect elsewhere in the New Testament.

Promises

He who calls you is faithful and he will do it. *(1 Thes. 5:24)*

There is little here to arouse resistance from modern readers. None of the words triggers a negative response, and for that very reason the sound may seep through our ears as smoothly as any pious platitude. But when we put this brief assurance under the microscope, a whole world of thought comes into view. The basic verb is in the present tense, signifying that the lord who calls is understood to be alive and well. This present time is defined by the bond between this congregation in Thessalonica (the *you* is plural) and its God. He has defined their present as the time of vocation. Whether one analyzes the syntax or the logic of the sentence, he will note a strong accent upon the adjective *faithful.* That adjective sustains the promise and invites reliance on the part of the congregation. It is assumed that this faithfulness brackets the entire span of the congregation's life: the call had introduced a very specific span of time; that span will end when God fulfills what he has promised. In remembering its beginning, the congregation is urged to anticipate this ending. During the interim its life is sustained not by its own faithfulness but by God's. This simple sentence, so polished and slender, summarizes both the inner dynamics and the outer world-scape of this congregation's calling. Its entire history is epitomized in a sentence that is readily intelligible and that appears at first sight to arouse few problems.

We note, however, that the sentence makes two blunt assertions about God: he "is faithful," "he will do it." These two assertions are not separable, for the faithfulness is to be measured by the doing, and the doing is the proof of the faithfulness. If the doing does not follow, the first claim is worthless; should the faithfulness evaporate, the doing could not be expected to follow, and the reason for the community's existence would vanish. So everything now depends on the promise "he will do it." To test the promise, three questions become relevant: (1) To what does this tiny word *it* refer? (2) What are the forces opposed to this doing? (3) What resources does God have at hand for accomplishing this *it?* When we consider the clues to the answers that are furnished in 1 Thessalonians, we are confronted with difficulties similar to those encountered in Mark 13. The previous verse located the *it* which God is expected to do: nothing less than the complete sanctification of this community "at the coming of our Lord Jesus Christ" (5:23). Moreover, the previous chapter appraises the forces opposed to this fulfilment: they include the whole range of heathen lusts, the unexpected deaths of brothers, and the confusions about the times and seasons. The forces which God has at his command to fulfill his promise seem to be entirely concentrated on the time of Christ's coming descent from heaven (4:15–17). It would seem that the community must have an unwavering trust in Christ's future power to overcome every adversary, though evidence of that power is quite invisible. Thus, although the form of the promise in 1 Thessalonians 5:24 is simpler, the fulfilment of that promise is no less problematic than in Mark.

Other capsule promises appear in the New Testament, and our concern with the more baroque cosmic images should not lead us to overlook more prosaic and concrete assurances. Here is a sampling:

— If we have died with him, we shall also live with him. (2 Tim. 2:11)

— Whether we live or die, we are the Lord's (Rom. 14:8).

— Humble yourself before the Lord and he will exalt you (James 4:10).

— Blessed is the man who endures trial, for when he has stood the test, he will receive the crown of life which God has promised to those who love him (James 1:12).

— We share in Christ if only we hold fast our first confidence to the end. (Heb. 3:14)

— Let us hold fast the confession of our hope without wavering, for he who promised is faithful. (Heb. 10:23)

— Be steadfast, immovable, always abounding in the work of the Lord, knowing that in the Lord your labor is not in vain. (1 Cor. 15:58)

— He who began a good work in you will bring it to completion at the day of Jesus Christ. (Phil. 1:6.)

Without major exception these promises place the community within the context of an agelong story that began and will end with the activity of God in Jesus Christ. That story gives a prominent place to the experience of conflict and suffering which has been provoked by that unique calling. The promises seek to persuade congregations that these conflicts are inescapable, and that they are, in fact, advance steps in the movement of the drama. Should followers try to incorporate their experience within the competing story of the world (and the temptation to do so was great) they would destroy their role in the story of Christ. It is because the conflict is due to the inherent incompatibility between the world's story and Christ's story that they ought to welcome the conflict as the context within which they were called to give "the confession of our hope."

There is an inner structure to the logic of these promises, and if we should X-ray that logic we would find four basic convictions:

1. The origin of the calling as the work of God must be

traced back not simply to the moment of conversion but beyond that to the beginning before all other beginnings, to an election "before the foundation of the world" (our symbol A).

2. The term of the calling, whether near or far, is traced ahead not simply to the death of the person called but to an end beyond all other endings, to a day of the Lord when God will be all in all (our symbol Z).

3. The present response to the calling, which covers a wide range of situations and duties, is seen as a way by which both individuals and congregations share in the sufferings and death of Christ (our symbol X).

4. Not only does this calling articulate a cluster of duties as an expression of gratitude to Christ, but it also makes accessible a reservoir of energies and competencies needed for their accomplishment, and it releases a vast range of joys and confidences that distinguishes the entire period of obedience (our symbol Y).

What we have noticed in the case of 1 Thessalonians 5:24 is true of these other capsules. The difficulties of interpretation inhere not in the metaphorical language used to describe the ultimate horizon (whether it be a moon that turns bloody or a love that never fails) but in the inherent incompatibilities between this calling and the "world" within which the calling must be vindicated. None of the promises can come true apart from radical sacrifices by the community or apart from radical shifts in the world's balances of power. In each of the epitomes, the ultimate issue is the validity of the calling rather than the symbolic descriptions of world's end, since in no case can the fulfillment of the promises come within the range of objective proofs.

Having examined these simpler promises we will now return to more difficult ones. The exploration is arranged in three stages.

—Because this promise in Mark 13:24–27 represents a Z-expectation we will look more closely at its relation to the X and Y components.

—Because the XYZ as an end-symbol corresponds to the

ABC as a beginning-symbol, we will look more closely at this relationship.

—Because early Christian thinking about both p and f symbols was conditioned by reflection on the X event, we will look more closely at that conditioning.

The Symbolism of the End

As we return to the analysis of Mark 13, where the eruption of successive catastrophes can so easily obscure the underlying logic of thought, we must not forget what we have learned about the vocation of this community and about the horizons of that vocation. With these in mind we should examine the chapter as a whole, with its sequence of seemingly disparate predictions.

There is a logic implicit in the position of this chapter within the Gospel of Mark. Consider the timing: this is a strategic moment in the story of Jesus' training of his disciples. Coming immediately before the Passion, it anticipates a reunion after that Passion. But even before that reunion, his suffering will place them under an almost intolerable stress. They will be subjected to fears, hostilities, deceptive illusions, panic; the very pressures which he overcame will produce on their part a frantic scattering. Mark turns this kaleidoscope slowly so that readers will see what it will be like to live as Jesus' elect after his death and before his return. If they are to vindicate his calling they must anticipate this spate of disasters and be ready to "stand." The time of their lives is here seen from a quite definite perspective; it reaches from his "recent" presence with them (13: 34–36) to his "speedy" return.

Consider also the geographical setting: these friends of Jesus stand on the Mount of Olives, overlooking the temple where he is about to be rejected by his people, and near the garden where he will almost immediately be arrested. The details of these predictions are shaped in part by his impending struggle and death. For example, his command for them to watch anticipates his ability to watch and their inability to do so a few hours later.[5] To the editor of the Gospel, this

chapter is much more than the Lord's final speech; it is a
message proclaimed by the cross itself, not only to these four
disciples but through them to all the elect (v. 37). It is his
Passion that actually determines the conditions and term of
their calling. (More on the relation of Z to X later.)

One would, of course, be unwise to treat the chapter as a
continuous line of argument, presented in a single speech of
Jesus and delivered on a single occasion. In all probability the
Marcan editor has assembled sayings which had circulated
separately during the decades following Jesus' death and
which had been shaped in part by the church's experience. By
collecting them and locating them at this point in his story,
Mark has given an awesome digest of the hazards of discipleship that had prevailed between Jesus' day and his own. Included are the following:

— the destruction of the oldest and holiest buildings
— the arrival of persuasive messianic pretenders
— the onset of wars, earthquakes, famine
— indictments and trials before sacred and secular courts
— betrayals by kinfolk and friends, hatred by all men
— a desolating sacrilege with vast tribulations
— darkened sun, moon, stars

Such an ominous sequence of terrors should be enough to
daunt the stoutest hearts. Yet these are presented as the normal circumstances that the disciples must expect to face in
doing their assigned work. Of course the motive for dwelling
on these horrors was not to dishearten them, for the events
themselves would take care of that; it was to prevent them from
being deceived and to keep them alert. The warnings spelled
out the kind of warfare they would need to wage, a warfare
which, in the idiom of Ephesians 6, would pit them against
demonic powers and not against flesh and blood. The types of
conflict would correspond to the various warnings: don't believe it . . . don't be alarmed . . . this is only the beginning
. . . this must first take place . . . watch.

When we ask why Mark (or Jesus) should have stressed such

grotesque predictions, our answers should include various factors. For one thing, dramatic imagery was demanded by the conviction that such things had not happened since "the beginning of creation" (v. 19). Unprecedented events call for unprecedented language. That same imagery served in a measure to objectify the inner agonies of the disciples as they struggled to fulfill their mission. Historical justifications for the use of hyperbolic analogies also existed, for, by the time Mark was writing, Christian communities in Jerusalem and Rome had already faced emergencies which made such predictions as these seem relatively mild. To them it was a source of encouragement that Jesus had not only endured such trials but had also forewarned his disciples: "See, I have told you all things beforehand" (v. 23).

Still another factor is important. Mark was well aware of the dangers of a martyr complex which induces a persecuted minority to feed on compensations craved by self-pity. He met those dangers by leading his readers into an ambush, for we find after the extreme apocalyptic cataclysms of vv. 1–27 a most unexpected anticlimax. Having prepared his readers for still more stunning developments he tells the parable of a fig tree, budding, as always, in springtime. And this is followed by a platitudinous command to stay awake. How ordinary and banal! It would seem that in his view the greatest danger to them comes not from cosmic dislocations but from drowsiness. And how would such dislocations, taken literally, have put them to sleep in the first place? We cannot avoid the conclusion that conventional apocalyptic imagery is being used here in a most unconventional way. The imagery discloses the invisible dimensions of the struggle in which Jesus was even then engaged. (One needs only to read the story of Gethsemane and Calvary to grasp the thrust of the cosmic metaphors.) It discloses also how much would depend upon the alertness of Jesus' disciples, not alone in the garden but even more in Mark's own day. The idiom is apocalyptic, but this strange vocation reverses all popular expectations concerning the character of messianic warfare.

This reversal, in fact, characterizes the entire mission and message of Jesus. This motif has been thrown into sharp relief in recent studies of the parables.

> If the last becomes first we have the story of Joseph. If the first becomes last we have the story of Job. But if the last becomes first *and* the first becomes last we have a polar reversal, a reversal of world as such. When the north pole becomes the south pole, and the south the north, a world is reversed and overturned, and we find ourselves standing firmly on utter uncertainty.[6]

We need to realize that the whole of Mark 13 is in some respects as figurative as are the parables of the seed in Mark 4. The shaking of the powers in heaven will take place as silently and inconspicuously as the budding of the fig tree. That is why it was only Jesus who noticed that sky-quake and why the disciples went to sleep during the catastrophe of chapter 14. That is why Mark preserved these stories for the sake of his own church, and why that church later canonized those stories. The reversal of all expectations concerning the end remains one of the permanent fruits of the tree on which Jesus was sacrificed. It is this X-event that forced a reshaping of all ideas concerning the Z-consummation.

How, then, does the understanding of the church's mission during the interim (the Y-period) affect these same traditions? We have already noted how the actual historical experiences of the church provided a commentary on the apocalyptic scenario. Let us add a comment on the importance of v. 10: "the gospel must first be preached to all nations." At first sight, this prediction seems quite out of place in this chamber of horrors. What does such a saying have to do with the anticipation of cosmic upheavals? Some interpreters conclude that its appearance here is quite accidental. Others suppose that its presence serves as a way of recognizing that in Mark's day the predictions had not come true, and that this saying is a way of postponing the predicted catastrophes until an unreal and remote future. Yet I am convinced that the verse is no alien intrusion, and that the editor had very good reasons for including the saying at this very point. The previous verse identifies the forum in which the gospel is to be preached: synagogues, governors, kings. The subsequent verse gives the setting in greater detail: they will be put on trial for their lives, when everything will hinge on whether or not they rely upon words provided by the Holy Spirit, the unseen "preacher." Mark was convinced, as was Paul, that the preaching of the good news would provoke the trials he predicted in such colorful language, and that only a witness given under such conditions would be able to show to enemies of the mission the divine power at work in the gospel. How could Jesus' victory over principalities and powers be conveyed except by current demonstrations of that victory? Again we should note the appropriate convergence of metaphors. A victory on the part of the disciples in their death struggle would signal a darkening of the same sun that was darkened on Good Friday, but the same victory would be as silent as spring's work in the fig tree. Only this master could require and determine this degree of alertness on the part of these servants. The vision of the Z-horizon is wholly fitting for the Y-vocation.

The whole chapter, in short, provides a succinct, if surrealist, transcript of what we have called the XYZ symbol. Placed within the period of activity, anxiety, and anguish (Y) that would be precipitated by that struggle, it promises an end to that struggle, not in cosmic disaster but in the return of the Lord and his reunion with his elect. The imagery is only a baroque conventional elaboration of the no less demanding promise of Philippians 1:6: "He who began a good work in you will bring it to completion at the day of Jesus Christ."

The Symbolism of the Beginning

No story can be fully told without including both its end and its beginning. No story of a vocation can be fully convincing apart from fundamental congruence between that beginning and that end. It has long been recognized that ancient apocalypses illustrated that congruence: visions of both horizons were shaped in the same studio. They provided answers to three questions concerning the beginning:

— What were God's basic intentions before the foundation of the world?
— What disturbances since then have distorted those intentions?
— What have been the long-term effects of those disturbances upon the present human situation?

It should be obvious that no living persons were present at that long-ago time; knowledge of absolute beginnings far exceeds the range of normal human experience. Yet the importance of the questions forces human imagination to press behind those normal boundaries; to do that the ablest of thinkers have had recourse to symbolic and mythical forms of expression. To be sure, such recourse may appear to cloak a confession of failure, but it often has produced a genuine liberation of the mind.

> Metaphorical theology could be a form of liberation theology *par excellence;* it might become liberating not in some programmatic but in a thoroughly performative sense, by setting free the *theos* of *logos* as well as the *logos* of *theos.* [7]

A deep-going exploration of the symbolisms expressed in the biblical visions of beginning and end may be found in Paul Ricoeur's recent writing, and we may well summarize some of his major theses.[8] This philosopher insists that any profound reflection concerning human experience "must embrace both an archaeology and an eschatology,"[9] since only this double horizon of genesis and apocalypse can give to history any sense of direction, orientation, and momentum.[10] To grasp this horizon, however, requires that thought move into the realm of mythical narrative; such narrative fulfills an essential function of clarifying "the concrete universal of human experience."[11] The universality that is embodied in the narrative makes it impossible to correlate mythical times with the historian's time-line or mythical space with the measurements of geographer or astronomer.[12] The mythical narrative can represent all times without destroying the fact that each person experiences only one particular time;[13] it tells the story of humankind without obscuring the story of each specific community, since each community retains its own anchorage in primordial and eschatological realities. It is characteristic of this mythical narrative to encapsulate the universal drama in the story of archetypal human figures, and to link the figure at the end to the figure at the beginning.

> The Fall of man cuts history in two, just as the coming of Christ cuts history in two. The two schemata are more and more superimposed like inverse images. A perfect and fabulous humanity precedes the Fall in the same way as humanity at the end of time succeeds to the manifestation of the archetypal man.[14]

In its perception of these archetypal figures, mythical narrative is characterized by its ability to embody the whole of reality in a single picture: "The supernatural, the natural and the psychological are not yet torn apart.[15] Any interpretation of the narrative that tears apart the existential from the cosmic, or the historical from the transcendent, destroys the essential integrity of the story and trivializes its significance.[16]

Though Ricoeur insists on this interdependence of the psychic and the ontic elements, he proceeds on the assumption that one can penetrate the primordial cosmic origins by way of analyzing psychic experience, and especially the experience of defilement, sin, and guilt. The human awareness of evil presupposes a prior goodness. "The evil is not symmetrical with the good. . . . However radical evil may be, it cannot be as powerful as goodness."[17] That same awareness presupposes that this primal goodness has been disrupted by a self-willed action, and that as a result of that disruption I have yielded myself "to slavery," to "the reign over myself of the power of evil."[18] "To sin is to yield," and in this yielding I confess that "a cosmic structure of evil" has attracted the support of "something of me."[19] The mythical narrative of the

Fall is therefore much more than symbolism of subjectivity, "of interiorized self-awareness." Evil is seen "as part of the history of being."[20] Imbedded in the experience of defilement, then, is the intuition that I have made a fateful transition (B) from my "essential nature" (A) to "an alienated history" (C).[21]

This same experience, of course, binds me to the experience of society as a whole; it is implicitly a recognition of "the concrete universality of human evil."[22] Only as an expression of man's solidarity in evil can the narrative prologue to history serve as a dramatic epitome of history. So the archetypal figure that stands at the beginning is able to condense "in an archetype of man everything which the believer experiences in a fugitive fashion and confesses in an allusive way."[23]

> By dividing the Origin into an origin of the goodness of the created and an origin of the wickedness in history the myth tends to satisfy the twofold confession of the Jewish believer, who acknowledges on the one hand the absolute perfection of God and, on the other hand, the radical wickedness of man. This twofold confession is the very essence of his repentance.[24]

The mythical narrative must express not only the actuality of individual fault, not only the communal dimensions of that fault, but also the perduring strength of the power that holds him captive. After the Fall, Adam is unable to return to the Garden. "Sin inhabits man more than man commits sin. It enters, abounds, reigns."[25] Human judgment can no longer be trusted, since good has been called evil and evil good. To be an adequate epitome of history the prologue must now picture an earth choked with thorns, animals turned into enemies, brother slaying brother, and work dogged by futility. The powers in the heavens have established a regime that challenges the power of God to free creation from the consequences of the fault, to free the captives of sin and death. Seen in its cosmic implications, then, the confession of sin says something about all things: all things have been created good, all things have been corrupted by sin, all things have been delivered over to captivity.

This analysis of the intrinsic structure and significance of mythical narratives indicates how biblical ideas of pre-existence may be understood. At the earliest horizon stands God, God alone. He alone is good and the source of life and goodness. All things are good at the moment of their creation. To know his name "is to know his purpose for all mankind from the beginning to the end."[26] It is to his primal power and goodness that the experience of fault points.

Reflection upon the mythical narrative includes various answers to the question of what things existed with God before the foundation of the world. Jews and Christians agreed on some of those answers: they viewed as primal such realities as life, light, the election of the people, the choice of the patriarchs, the messianic age, even the act of repentance. Some answers given by the Jewish community were rejected by Christians; they could not agree to assigning to the realm of pre-existence such institutions as the Torah and the Temple, the Sabbath and circumcision. Some answers given by Christians were rejected by the synagogues: Jesus as the Messiah, as the *Logos* that was with God before all things, as one who existed before Abraham, the kingdom of God, the elect community, the bread of heaven, the power of the Holy Spirit, the love of God. Christians believed that Christ had revealed to them things hidden from the foundation of the world. This revelation included the vast significance of the cross. Because the Lamb had been slain from the foundation of the world, that one sacrifice somehow included the blood of all the prophets that had been shed from the foundation of the world and all that would be shed before the end.

Though Jewish and Christian answers concerning pre-existence differed, those answers reflected a common sensitivity to the symbolism of origins. Moreover there was a common awareness of the importance of these answers, inasmuch as the shape of thinking about the epilogue to history corresponded so closely to thinking about the prologue. This was inescapable for Christians since the resurrection was "always associated by them with the imminent renewal of the creation as a whole."[27] No story of a future consummation would carry conviction unless it completed the story of the creation of all things.

> The resurrection story would be stultified if the horizons of world-drama were forfeited, that is, its Jewish apocalyptic structure. The resurrection had to do with the course and the goal of the world-process, its throes and its consummation.[28]

We return, then, to Ricoeur's conviction that human experience requires a double horizon of genesis and apocalypse. Both end and beginning are implicit in the same awareness of fault, inasmuch as that awareness both presupposes an earlier transition from innocence to guilt and anticipates a future transition from guilt to purification.[29] It is this anticipation that invites the act of penitence. In such action, the penitent responds to the plenitude of redemptive forces that break from the future into the present.

One may therefore visualize this double horizon in the shape of an all-inclusive *chiasmus*. The captivity consequent on Adam's sin (C) is overcome by a fresh infusion of God's power that takes captivity captive (X); penitents thereby receive the gracious gift of a forgiveness for their sin (B) that frees them for authentic obedience (Y); thus the road is opened to Paradise Regained, where the Creator's life is again shared fully with his people (A, Z). Implicit in the psychic experience of sin and forgiveness is the primordial ontology of alienation and the eschatological ontology of reconciliation; this ontology, however, can only find expression in mythical narrative in which, at each of the six stages, the adjective *all* bespeaks the inclusiveness of the categories.

I have just used the technical term *chiasmus*, which calls for a word of explanation. The term *chiasmus* has normally been used to characterize literary forms which can be diagrammed in the shape of the Greek letter *chi*. Among the earlier books dealing with this form is one by Nils W. Lund.[30] The literary form is a case of inverted parallelism, in which the first item in a series is like the last, and the second is like the next to the last, etc.; e.g., whoever saves his life (a) will lose it (b), and whoever loses his life (b) will save it (a). As Professor Lund insisted, this pattern not only expresses Hebrew thinking, but it helps to shape it.[31] Among the features of this style of thinking are these: the center always functions as the turning point; identical ideas occur at the extremes and at the center, with the focus of thought shifting from the center to the extremes.[32] If I am right, the mythical symbolism embodied in the schema of ABC/XYZ illustrates chiastic thinking and also expresses the conviction that this pattern belongs to the very structures of historical existence.

We return now to Mark 13 to see if any new implications emerge from the text. We have already noted that these teachings reflect the conviction of the saving efficacy of Jesus' death. In the saying "I have told you all things beforehand" (v. 23), that adverb *beforehand* refers to the Passover feast and its sacrifice. Mark tells the story in such a way as to locate in Gethsemane and on Golgotha events that disclose both the alienation and the reconciliation of all things (X). In fact, Jesus' death establishes the way in which his words transcend the story of heaven and earth (v. 31). It may not be wrong to relate that death to various segments of chapter 12: it represents God's answer to Israel's rebellions (vv. 8–11); it expresses the presence and power of the God of the patriarchs (vv. 26, 27); it celebrates the fulfillment of the greatest commandment (vv. 28–34); it delivers Israel from false ideas of David's kingdom (vv. 35–37) and from false interpretations of Scripture (vv. 38–40); it reverses human measurements of religious devotion (vv. 41–44); it even shows how expendable are the most sacred institutions (13:1–2). Whether or not these allusions were present in Mark's mind, there is no doubt that his narrative centers on the significance of the cross as a pivot of God's dealing with his people and as God's way of overcoming their rebellions.

We have also noted how the Marcan apocalypse defines the mission of Jesus' followers during the interim between his death and theirs (the Y-period). They are called to give their witness to his death by facing and defeating a similar spate of temptations and obstacles. They will proclaim God's news in forums like his as they stand trial before governors and kings and as they enable the Spirit of the new age to speak through them (v. 11). The sin of Cain, repeated in their own stories, will become a sign of this new age. Facing tribulations without precedent since the beginning of creation, their victories will constitute a redemptive reversal of the stories of Adam and Eve, Cain and Abel, and the generation of Noah. This narrative of the current interim has been shaped by three major factors: by conventional apocalyptic descriptions of primordial rebellions and messianic expectations, by communal memories of Jesus' death and resurrection, and by the cumulative experience of the Christian community during several decades of persecution.

We should now look again at the symbolic description of the Z-event in Mark 13:24–27. Here the most spectacular prediction has to do with the powers of the heavens. Does the chiastic mode of thinking extend to this prediction? I think it does. When this story was told to a Christian congregation, it would have recalled to their minds the Genesis story of the fourth day, when the heavenly bodies were created to rule the day and the night.

> And God made the two great lights . . . he made the stars
> . . . to separate the light from the darkness. *(Gen. 1:16f.)*

The Marcan prophecy presupposes that these powers, originally good, have been corrupted, and that this corruption must be overcome if creation is to return to the primal goodness. The powers entrenched in the heavens must be shaken. The stages in redemption must reverse the order in the stages of creation. The earlier paragraphs in chapter 13 illustrate something of this reverse order: the destruction of the temple, the erosion of national securities and identities, the apparent extermination of God's people by their enemies, an abysmal sacrilege that threatens the survival of human life. Only after the story pictures this threat to all flesh (the fifth and sixth days of creation) do the works of the fourth day come into view. Only after God has over- come the corruption of the works of this fourth day, can he restore the initial goodness to his creation. It should not be forgotten that the heavenly luminaries, created on the fourth day, had been preceded by the creation of light on the first day.[33] So this whole parade of cosmic catastrophes is prelude to the restoration of the primordial glory of life and light which had attended God's first word.

> Then they will see the Son of man coming in clouds with great power and glory.

No doubt Mark identified this figure with Jesus, the returning master of the parable, and that identification must have changed the content of the traditional symbolism. The clouds indicate his heavenly origin and status, his transcendence of times and places. It is fitting that the shaking of all other heavenly powers (v. 24) should be done by one who had been exalted to heaven from earth.[34] In this context the adjective *great* is a conventional tag that refers to apocalyptic expec- tations,[35] but the noun *power* has been redefined by the kind of authority exercised by Jesus during his earthly min- istry.[36] So, too, while his glory excels the glory of sun and moon, in typical apocalyptic style, the earlier chapters in Mark have served to reverse the normal conceptions of the divine glory. In any case, the darkening of sun and moon provides a hyperbolic foil for stressing the transformations wrought by this Son of man. His glory is God's glory which in the end he will share with the elect.[37]

So the reference to the Son of man is incomplete without its sequel:

> And then he will send out his angels and gather his elect from the four winds, from the ends of earth to the ends of heaven.

The climax of the narrative of cosmic upheaval is to be found here, in the fulfillment of the Messiah's concern for those whom he has called. They are to be gathered from all directions and from all generations; their reunion will represent an authentic transcendence of time and space. They have been scattered by the centrifugal force of trials and persecutions; he will furnish whatever centripetal force is needed to bring them together in a fulfillment of his vocation and of theirs. Those who have been called of God from before the sun was created will be united again after the sun has been darkened. The master's promise of this gathering is itself a word that will survive the demise of heaven and earth (v. 31). In trusting that promise Mark's readers responded to a reality which they believed was more ultimate, as an expression of God's purpose, than the sun, moon, or stars. Mark was appealing to these readers, not to modern readers.

To sum up, we suggest that the promises of Mark 13 articulate two deeply rooted convictions involved in preaching the gospel to all nations (v. 10). In the first place, if the Son of man has won a victory over the heavenly powers that through sin and death have held men in thrall, that victory must be vindicated in "tribulations" and described in images awesome enough and inclusive enough to embrace the whole of human history. In the second place, those tribulations must be presented as inherent in a promise that beyond the worst conceivable prospect on earth is a God who cares for those whom he calls and who has the power to redeem a community "from the four winds." To limit the resurrection of the Son of man to something less than cosmic dimensions, or to limit the vocation of the church in similar fashion, would be to deny that this resurrection and this vocation were acts of God. Of course a fidelity to those dimensions necessitated the adoption and modification of a mythological narrative, but this narrative conveyed "a universality, a temporality, and an ontological significance to the immediate experience of sin and forgiveness."[38] Mark 13 adds to that basic experience of "sin and forgiveness" the experience of receiving from the Risen Lord a vocation to proclaim the gospel to all nations.

Transformation of the Symbolism

It does not require great ingenuity to recognize problematic elements in such a narrative. The implicit claim to universality, by way of the shaking of heavenly powers, rules out any confirmation by appeal to objective evidence. By contrast, the assertion of temporal relevance to a particular generation (v. 30) puts this promise in the position of being the hostage of the historian: if the promise seems to have been fulfilled, its origin can be traced to a period later than that fulfillment; if it is not fulfilled, the credibility of the prophet is destroyed. In either case he loses. Moreover, how does one test or vindicate the ontological ultimacy of the specific vocation of a specific community, as expressed in the concluding parable (vv. 34ff.)? Since this promise is stated in the symbolic language of that community, it may not be translatable into an external idiom. It requires exegesis, yet every effort at interpretation may add to the confusion and controversy. It would seem that such a vocational horizon cannot be objectified in knowledge that is subject to external verification. This covenant between this master and his servants remains anchored in their mutual concerns and in their subsequent autobiographies.[39]

If we are to grasp its meanings to them, we must do what is virtually impossible: by way of their language we must penetrate the secret place where they carry on their dialogue, for this is a dialogue between this particular master and this particular group of disciples. In that dialogue, as we have noted above, the problematic elements were located not in the credibility of the prophecies to later readers, but in the stress and strain of a most demanding vocation. This master was involved in a struggle of which Gethsemane would be the measure, and we have noticed that Mark kept that struggle constantly in view in chapter 13. His followers would soon be engaged in a continuation of that same struggle, as soon, that is, as the Risen Lord should renew their commission.

In the context of that mutual calling, we should not overlook some apparently insignificant phrases which show how greatly conventional apocalyptic language has been modified. One

such phrase is *for my sake*. It was "for my sake" that they would
stand on trial before governors and kings (v. 9); "for my
name's sake," that they would be hated by all (v. 13). Every
situation pictured in the chapter is a test of their love for a very
particular person. Even when false leaders appeared with their
plausible messages to deceive his disciples, those leaders
would appeal to his "name" (v. 6), so that only greater devotion to his way of proclaiming the gospel would enable followers to detect the fraud. Watchfulness in time of crisis or of
boredom would be the best proof of loyalty to this crucified
Messiah. Nor should we neglect to stress the importance of his
love for them, as evidenced by the indestructibility of his
words (v. 31). In a sense the parade of catastrophes which fills
the chapter discloses the realism of his promise: in their lives
there would be incontrovertible evidence of hatred by men but
no visible evidence of his love for them . . . until the very end.
They would face situations entirely comparable to that which
evoked his prayer in Gethsemane, his cry from the cross. Only
in their case they would have as a resource his promise of a
time when he would gather his elect. The stars falling from
heaven give their witness to the realism of this promise; their
crucified teacher gives his witness to its dependability. Their
common horizon is the horizon of their mutual love.

> The ultimate may be incomprehensible by thought just because
> only love can embrace it, since love itself is incomprehensible
> in its power and infinite in its extent.[40]

Professor Kroner's words suggest that the power and the glory
with which the Son of man comes (v. 26) should be understood
as the power and glory of his love, a love disclosed in the cross,
and a love that will be disclosed in their later crosses, and
therefore the love of the community that will be gathered by
the holy angels. The prediction of the darkened sun becomes
a measure of the universal range and the transcendent power
of this love; in this case Mark 13:24–27 as a description of the
Z-event becomes an appropriate way of confessing that the

God who created all things (A-event) is the God of love. In that case, Søren Kierkegaard's reflections on 1 Corinthians 13:7 become applicable to Mark 13: "Love believeth all things—and yet is never deceived"; "Love hopeth all things—and yet is never put to shame."[41] I have long believed that those essays are among the best explications of early Christian eschatology in the history of exegesis.

So the vocation of love, a vocation shared by the Elect One with his elect disciples, constitutes an essential clue to the substance of these promises in Mark 13. But why have interpreters failed to give this clue due weight? There are many reasons. One is the inclination to view the symbolism from sophisticated modern vantage points or to interpret it as something borrowed from Jewish extremists by early Christians without basic modifications. But another reason is the refusal to understand the essential bond between the love of Christ and suffering for his sake. It would be a travesty on the gospel to picture the triumph of Christ's love apart from the resistance to it on the part of "all men" (v. 13). His love for the world produced hatred by the world; only so could it mark the redemption of the world. The apocalyptic imagery of Mark 13 is relevant to preserving this paradoxical mystery; how else can one confess the universality of the gospel of suffering?[42]

This factor may help us to grasp why a chief thrust of this chapter deals with a division within the community of disciples over competing prophets. There will be true prophets and false, and the latter will present the more impressive credentials. In fact, it will be false prophets who exploit the conventional apocalyptic excitements, appealing to wars, earthquakes, and famine as signs to corroborate their warnings. It will be they who feed the anxieties and apprehensions of the community and who see on every hand signs of imminent cataclysm (v. 22). Though they will come "in Christ's name," they will not use his teachings to calm fears or to steady nerves. They will not follow his example nor accept the hazards of watching with him. They will not devote themselves to the tasks he assigned them. The more strident becomes their shouting, the more must disciples quietly heed Jesus' warning: "do not believe it" (v. 21).

All this shows how inherently ambiguous are apocalyptic expectations as such; it shows also how that ambiguity can be resolved only by the test of vocation. It is the vocation of the Son of man, completed in his Passion, which gives a realistic content to this dialogue. It is the vocation of his elect, called to stand before governors and kings for his sake (v. 9), which defines the boundary between true prophets and false. Disciples will discover how radically their vocation reverses their previous expectations concerning "the sign when all these things are to be accomplished" (v. 4). They will also discover that this question should be asked and answered privately, within the frame of dialogue with him, as they stand with him on the Mount of Olives, immediately before the Passover. It is this date, this place, and this personnel which determine the inner meanings of this dialogue.[43]

Here we must state as bluntly and as clearly as possible one implication of this study of Mark 13, for it applies equally well to the other apocalyptic promises of Jesus. These promises are intended *only* for those who understand and who accept their vocation under Him. Interpreters have been prone to ask the wrong questions: Have these predictions come true? Are they still to come true? Were they intended only for that ancient situation or only for some crisis still to come? No. These teachings were given only to the "vocationed." People who have not joined that company have no right to exploit these teachings, whether or not they claim to belong to a family called Christian. The prior question is one of the vocation of the Son of man and the vocation of those who live in and through him (1 Cor. 8:6). It is the horizoning of *their* calling that is described in these verses. No one else is qualified to share in that intimate dialogue.

To be sure, even they will experience many difficulties, intellectual as well as practical. Are they troubled by the idiom of a darkened sun? Of course they are. So they should ponder the significance of the darkness that fell on Friday noon (15:33).

Are they baffled by the prediction that the heavenly powers will be shaken (13:25)? Of course they cannot avoid being bewildered. Yet they can recognize that this prediction belongs to the same order as the assurance that Jesus would be exalted to "the right hand of Power" (14:62), an assurance which the high priest recognized to be the height of blasphemy. The shaking of the sun and moon are intended to attest the reality of that exaltation. This brings us to the realization that the text of Mark 13:24–27, which we have dubbed the most problematic paragraph in the most problematic chapter, is simply a faithful pointer to the problem posed by the death and exaltation of Jesus. It is an intrinsic part of a vision of all creation, from the first sunup to the last sundown, as comprehended within the purpose of God as revealed in Jesus. In sum, then, the promise to gather the elect is a Marcan parallel to the equally dramatic, and equally problematic, promise in the Gospel of John:

> When I am lifted up from the earth I will draw all men to myself." *(12:32; cf. also 11:51f.)*

Notes

Part I

[1]Hugh Kenner, *The Pound Era*, p. 39, cited in J. D. Crossan, *In Parables* (New York: Harper & Row, 1973), p. 2.

Chapter 1

[1]Wallace Stevens, from "Addresses to the Academy of Fine Ideas," *The Collected Poems of Wallace Stevens* (New York: Knopf, 1967), p. 259.

[2]For a development of the concept that the base line of religious experience may be found in a person's efforts to discern "the inner relation" of each day's happenings "to the totality of things and the whole of experience," cf. R. Kroner, *Culture and Faith* (Chicago: University of Chicago, 1951), pp. 185ff.

[3]Karl Rahner, *Theological Investigations*, vol. 4 (New York: Seabury, 1974), p. 331.

[4]Recently Robert Bellah has observed that "behind every literal fact is an unfathomable depth of implication and meaning" and that when that depth is cut off a person experiences "a kind of sleep or death" (*The Broken Covenant* [New York: Seabury, 1975], p. 72).

[5]Many readers may be quite unconscious of the degree to which vocation, in the qualitative sense used in this book, applies to them. Although in this chapter I use the term in a general sense, my use is influenced by biblical and Christian traditions. Those who wish to examine the biblical roots of this idea are referred to my essay in J. O. Nelson, ed., *Work and Vocation* (New York: Harper, 1954), pp. 32–81.

[6]In what follows I ascribe to the sense of vocation what J. H. Newman ascribed to the mind: "[The mind] makes everything in some sort lead to everything else; it would communicate the image of the

whole to every separate portion, till that whole becomes in imagination like a spirit, everywhere pervading and penetrating its component parts, and giving them one definite meaning" (*The Idea of a University* [London: Basil Montagu Pickering, 1873], pp. 137–40). More recent experience has made us quite skeptical whether universities are actually fulfilling the role envisaged by Newman. A "multiversity" can destroy any such "image of the whole" and in so doing can dissolve any strong sense of vocation.

[7] *Markings* (New York: Knopf, 1964), p. 205.

[8] F. Buechner, *Alphabet of Grace* (New York: Seabury, 1970), pp. 21f.

[9] Quoted by R. Bellah, in R. E. Richey and D. G. Jones, eds., *American Civil Religion* (New York: Harper & Row, 1974), p. 256.

[10] Theodore Spencer, "For an April Birthday," in *An Act of Life* (Cambridge: Harvard University, 1944), p. 80.

[11] Ibid., p. 81.

[12] *New York Times Book Review*, November 9, 1975, p. 1.

[13] Ibid.

[14] Spencer, from "Heritage," in *An Act of Life*, p. 28.

[15] N. Mandelstam, *Hope Against Hope* (New York: Athenaeum, 1972), p. 143.

[16] *Letters and Papers from Prison* (London: SCM, 1953), p. 175.

[17] Buechner, *Alphabet of Grace*, p. 75.

[18] One of the first observers to trace the effects of this commuting on a person's self-image was Eugen Rosenstock-Huessy, in *The Christian Future* (New York: Harper, 1946), pp. 20ff.

[19] T. Berry, "Mao Tse-Tung: The Long March," *Cross Currents* 25 (1975): 2.

[20] The struggle between surrender and defiance in the case of American churches is well described in P. Berger, *A Rumor of Angels* (New York: Doubleday, 1960), chaps. 1 and 2.

[21] Dorothy Canfield Fisher, in her *Vermont Tradition*, speaks of her memories as reaching back two centuries to 1763 (Boston: Little, Brown 1953), p. 3.

[22] J. M. Gustafson, *Theology and Christian Ethics* (Philadelphia: United Church, 1974), p. 244.

[23] Another appraisal of this problem is presented in my study, *The Kingdom and the Power* (Philadelphia: Westminster, 1950), pp. 20–30.

[24] Spencer, from "Heritage," in *An Act of Life*, p. 35.

[25] Poets frequently help us to see unsuspected correlations; for example, a hymn of E. Farjean:

> *Morning has broken*
> *Like the first morning.*
> *Blackbird has spoken*
> *Like the first bird.*
> *Praise for the singing*
> *Praise for the morning.*
> *Praise for them, springing*
> *Fresh from the Word.*

(*Pilgrim Hymnal* [Boston: Pilgrim, 1968], no. 38.)

[26]See Stephen Crites, "Figures of Things to Come," paper delivered on April 16, 1977, at the American Theological Society.

[27]From "The Labyrinth," in *Collected Poems*, by W. H. Auden, ed. Edward Mendelson (New York: Random House; London: Faber and Faber, 1945), p. 10.

[28]Auden, from "Kairos and Logos," in *Collected Poems*, p. 15.

[29]Russell Baker, "O Zone," *New York Times*, March 2, 1975, section 6, part 1, p. 6.

[30]Similar irony is conveyed by a cartoon in *Punch*, which pictures, in details reminiscent of Dürer, the four horsemen of Revelation 6. One of the horsemen is asking his companion: "Is this your first Apocalypse?" Even in spite of the irony, of course, there is truth in the notion of the recurring relevance of such a "final" symbol as that of Death.

[31]Auden, from "For the Time Being," in *Collected Poems*, p. 411.

Part II

[1]P. Ricoeur, *The Symbolism of Evil* (Boston: Beacon, 1967), p. 171.

[2]Roger Hazelton, "Theology and Metaphor," *Religion in Life* 46 (1977), pp. 18ff.

Chapter 2

[1]J. Moltmann, *The Crucified God* (New York: Harper & Row, 1974), p. 124.

[2]See P. S. Minear, "Jesus' Audiences According to Luke," *Novum Testamentum* 16 (1974): 81–109.

[3]In an earlier book, *To Heal and to Reveal: The Prophetic Vocation According to Luke* (New York: Seabury, 1976), I have explored the distinctive language of these prophets (chaps. 1–3), together with their vocational training by Jesus (chaps. 4–7). Although written inde-

pendently, that book and this one supplement each other.

⁴R. Hazelton, *Religion in Life* 46 (1977), p. 13.

⁵So prevalent are the antithetical metaphors that it is unusual to find a metaphor without its antithesis. When that happens, certain questions must be raised. What, for example, is the antithesis to the reference to the empty tomb? Whatever antithesis we arrive at, we must ask whether that antithesis displays a basic kinship with the other twin analogies. Is the discovery of the empty tomb a feature essential to the others? Did the debates between believers and nonbelievers center on the credibility of an empty tomb or on some other feature of the story? The interpretation of many antitheses becomes a test of adequacy of each separate witness.

⁶For further explication, see below chapter 5.

⁷Hans Frei has fully documented the failure of modern criticism to recognize and preserve this narrative character of biblical thought. He calls this failure "the great reversal." Interpretation "became a matter of fitting the biblical story into another world with another story rather than incorporating the world into the biblical story" (*The Eclipse of Biblical Narrative* [New Haven: Yale University, 1974], pp. 130f.).

⁸Crossan, *In Parables*, p. 13.

⁹Ibid., p. 18.

¹⁰R. W. Jensen, *Story and Promise* (Philadelphia: Fortress, 1973), p. 48.

¹¹W. Marxsen, in C. F. D. Moule, ed., *The Significance of the Message of the Resurrection for Faith in Jesus Christ* (London: SCM, 1968), pp. 38–40.

¹²J. Jeremias, *New Testament Theology* (London: SCM, 1971), vol. 1, p. 52.

¹³J. V. Taylor, *The Go-Between God* (Philadelphia: Fortress, 1973), p. 87.

¹⁴See below, chapter 3.

¹⁵J. Moltmann, *Crucified God*, p. 37.

¹⁶M. Barth, *The Broken Wall* (Philadelphia: Judson, 1959), p. 54.

¹⁷See below, chapter 3.

¹⁸See below, chapter 4.

¹⁹See below, chapters 5 and 6.

²⁰*Eclipse of Biblical Narrative*, pp. 137ff.

²¹E. Dickinson, *Poems* (Boston: Little, Brown, 1930), pp. 195–96.

Chapter 3

[1]Amos N. Wilder, *Theopoetic* (Philadelphia: Fortress, 1976), pp. 52–53.

[2]Few modern thinkers have been so aware of the radical implications of this event as Søren Kierkegaard. One of the many possible citations from his *Journals* is sufficient evidence:

> Socrates did not possess the true ideal, nor had he any notion of sin, nor that man's salvation required a crucified God: the watchword of his life therefore could not be: "the world is crucified to me and I to the world." He therefore retained irony which simply expresses his superiority to the world's folly. But for a Christian irony is not enough, it can never answer to the terrible truth that salvation means that God is crucified, though irony can still be used for some time in Christendom, to arouse people.

(*The Journals of Søren Kierkegaard* [New York: Oxford University, 1938], p. 403, entry no. 1122.)

[3]I have used the RSV translation, which here is altogether too bland to express the strong Greek exclamation. One might almost render it: "God strike me down if I should rely on anything else but the cross."

[4]H. Sasse, in G. Kittel, ed., *Theological Dictionary of the New Testament*, vol. 3, p. 888.

[5]J. Moltmann, *Crucified God*, p. 40.

[6]R. C. Tannehill, *Dying and Rising with Christ* (Berlin: Topelmann, 1966), p. 70.

[7]Ibid., p. 71.

[8]Fr. Rinaldi, *La Scuola Cattolica* 100 (1972): 16–47, an article digested in *Internationale Zeitschriftenschau für Bibelwissenschaft* 20 (1973–1974): 137.

[9]G. S. Duncan, *The Epistle to the Galatians* (London: Hodder & Stoughton, 1934), p. 191.

[10]J. H. Ropes, *The Singular Problem of the Epistle to the Galatians* (Cambridge: Harvard University, 1929), p. 42.

[11]W. F. Arndt and F. W. Gingrich, *Greek-English Lexicon of the New Testament* (Chicago: University of Chicago, 1957), p. 447.

[12]R. Bultmann, *Theology of the New Testament*, vol. 1 (New York: Scribner, 1951), p. 257.

[13]An extended critique of this feature of Bultmann's thought, along with his rejoinder to it, may be found in C. W. Kegley, ed., *The Theology of Rudolf Bultmann* (New York: Harper & Row, 1966), pp. 65–82, 265–68.

[14]A case in point is to be noted in contemporary public discussions concerning Christians who have been born again. Endless and mindless palaver takes place over those who confess to a "second" birth. Instead of asking for evidences of such rebirth we might better ask *how many times* a person has died, and whether he has died to the "world," in the sense of the Galatians text. Birth without dying is Christian nonsense, and so is new creation without crucifixion.

[15]Crossan, *In Parables*, p. 31.

[16]G. Schneider, *Trier Theologische Zeitung* 68 (1959): 257–70; see digest in *New Testament Abstracts* 4 (1959–1960): 151.

[17]P. Stuhlmacher, *Evangelische Theologie* 27 (1967): 1–35; see digest in *New Testament Abstracts* 11 (1966–1967): 335.

[18]Carl Braaten, *Christ and Counter-Christ* (Philadelphia: Fortress, 1972), p. 32.

[19]N. Clark, *Interpreting the Resurrection* (London: SCM, 1967), p. 98.

[20]G. Fackre, *Andover Newton Theological Seminary Quarterly* 16 (1975): 157.

[21]Tykhon is cited in N. Gorodetzky, *The Humiliated Christ in Modern Russian Thought* (London: SPCK, 1938), p. 104. Much interest lately has centered in the rise of a charismatic movement in American churches. The degree to which such a movement is grounded in the triple crucifixion of Galatians 6:14 becomes a dependable test of its authenticity.

Chapter 4

[1]Braaten, *Christ and Counter-Christ*, p. 17.

[2]Taylor, *Go-Between God*, p. 70.

[3]It is true that today many scholars deny that Paul himself wrote this letter. There are many cogent reasons for such denial, though I have never been wholly persuaded by them. For the purposes of this chapter, however, the issue is relatively unimportant, first, because the unquestioned Pauline letters provide ample evidence for the major points, and second, because, even if pseudonymous, Ephesians would merit full respect as an unchallenged part of the canon of Scripture.

[4]*Religious Studies Review* 2 (July 1976): 15.

[5]*The Roots of Pagan Anti-Semitism in the Ancient World* (Leiden: Brill, 1975).

[6]Hare, *Religious Studies Review* 2:16.

[7]Cf. P. Ricoeur, *The Conflict of Interpretations* (Evanston: Northwestern University, 1974), p. 23.

[8]On this prophetic role, cf. my *To Heal and to Reveal.*

[9]See C. Masson, *L'Epitrè de Paul aux Ephesiens* (Neuchatêl: Delachaux et Niestlè, 1953), p. 175.

[10]A succinct summary of the work of these powers is given by G. Fackre:

> [They] express themselves in nature and history, in the depths of the self and in the structures of society. At the crucifixion they are at work in the institutions of political, military and ecclesiastical power, and in the captivity of the people to the idols and passions of the hour. . . . Thus both human-beings-in-sin and the powers-in-evil share complicity in Golgotha.

(*Andover Newton Theological Seminary Quarterly* 16 [1975]: 150.)

[11]See Gordon Rupp, *Last Things First* (Philadelphia: Fortress, 1964), p. 34.

[12]Taylor, *Go-Between God,* p. 118.

Chapter 5

[1a]J. Louis Martyn, "Glimpses into the History of the Johannine Community," *Ephemerides Theologicae Lovanienses,* 1977, p. 157.

[1b]Rudolf Augstein, *Jesus Son of Man* (New York: Urizen Books, 1977), p. 12.

[2]As a sampling of other definitions the following may be mentioned:

—to heal, to exorcize demons, to announce God's Kingdom (Lk. 10:8f.)

—to preach repentance and forgiveness of sins to all nations (Lk. 24:47)

—to feed the hungry, to clothe the naked, to visit prisoners . . . (Matt. 25:31ff.)

—to keep the commandments of God and to bear witness to Jesus (Rev. 12:17)

—to imitate those who through faith and endurance inherit the promises (Heb. 6:12)

—to make disciples of all nations, baptizing and teaching (Matt. 28:16ff.)

—to turn to God from idols and to await his Son from heaven (1 Thes. 1:9f.)

—to be built into a spiritual house, to be a holy priesthood, to offer spiritual sacrifices (1 Pet. 2:5)

I have attempted to present the entire New Testament picture in an essay in *Missiology* 5 (1977), pp. 13–37.

[3]Cf. my forthcoming essay, "The Beloved Disciple," in *Novum Testamentum.*

[4]See E. Hoskyns, *The Fourth Gospel* (London: Faber & Faber, 1940), p. 554.

[5]See C. K. Barrett, *The Gospel According to St John* (London: SPCK, 1955), p. 312; R. E. Brown, *The Gospel According to John I–XII* (New York: Doubleday, 1966), p. 396; Hoskyns, *Fourth Gospel*, p. 378.

[6]See R. Hazelton, *Blaise Pascal: The Genius of His Thought* (Philadelphia: Westminster, 1974), p. 136.

[7]See my essay, "The Idea of Incarnation in I John," *Interpretation* 24 (1970): 291–302.

[8]Evidence for this interpretation may be found in my essay, "We Don't Know Where," *Interpretation* 30 (1976): 125–39.

[9]From "For the Time Being," in *The Collected Poetry*, p. 447.

[10]From "Two Tramps in Mud Time," in *The Poetry of Robert Frost*, ed. Edward Connery Lathem. Copyright © 1964 by Lesley Frost Ballantine. Copyright © 1969 by Holt, Rinehart and Winston. Reprinted by permission of the Estate of Robert Frost, Jonathan Cape Ltd., and Holt, Rinehart and Winston, Publishers.

Chapter 6

[1]N. W. Lund, *Chiasmus in the New Testament* (Chapel Hill: University of North Carolina, 1942), p. 29. This chapter was one of the Lund Memorial Lectures. Its use of chiastic patterns to illuminate the early Christian vision of creation, old and new, represents an extension of Professor Lund's thought but is not, I trust, incompatible with it.

[2]B. Pascal, *Pensées* (New York: Random House, 1941), p. 264, no. 739. I am indebted for this reference to R. Hazelton, *Blaise Pascal*, p. 170.

[3]Cf. N. Perrin, *Jesus and the Language of the Kingdom* (Philadelphia: Fortress, 1976), pp. 77f.

4"Marxist Ecclesiology and Biblical Criticism," in *Journal of the History of Ideas* 37 (1976): 93–110.

5See R. H. Lightfoot, *The Gospel Message of St Mark* (Oxford: Clarendon, 1950), pp. 48–59.

6Crossan, *In Parables*, p. 55.

7R. Hazelton, *Religion in Life* 46 (1977), p. 17.

8*Symbolism of Evil* (New York: Harper & Row, 1967); *The Conflict of Interpretations* (Evanston: Northwestern University, 1974).

9*Conflict*, p. 333.

10Ibid., p. 293.

11Ibid.

12*Symbolism*, p. 162.

13Ibid., pp. 163f.

14*Conflict*, pp. 276f.

15*Symbolism*, p. 167.

16*Conflict*, pp. 308f.

17*Symbolism*, p. 156.

18Ibid.

19Ibid., p. 259.

20*Conflict*, p. 309.

21*Symbolism*, p. 170.

22Ibid., p. 241.

23*Conflict*, p. 283.

24*Symbolism*, p. 243.

25*Conflict*, pp. 282f.

26B. S. Childs, *The Book of Exodus* (Philadelphia: Westminster, 1974), p. 119.

27Wilder, *Theopoetic*, p. 95.

28Ibid., p. 99.

29*Conflict*, pp. 293f.

30*Chiasmus in the New Testament.*

31Ibid., p. 29.

32Ibid., pp. 40f.

33The reader may of course question whether Mark (or Jesus) consciously intended to shape this prediction of the end to parallel inversely the events in the Genesis story of creation. Yet it can hardly be denied that this prediction of a darkened sun is a conscious adaptation of a conventional Hebraic idiom that conveyed two central motifs: (1) God's inclusive judgment upon the realm of human rebellions as a whole (Is. 13:10; Ezek. 32:7–8; Joel 2:10, 31; 3:15; Amos

8:9; Rev. 6:12–14); (2) God's own role as the sun (Ps. 84:11) who is wholly capable of providing such light for his people that they no longer have need of the heavenly bodies (Is. 60:19–20; Rev. 21:23; 22:5). The prophets typically used this idiom to stress the present time as "the moment of truth" confronting God's people in "the valley of decision." Considering the pervasiveness of this biblical idiom it is ironic that modern Christians who consider themselves most loyal to the Bible should be so inflexibly literalistic in their interpretation of this idiom.

[34]Cf. my book, *Christian Hope and the Second Coming* (Philadelphia: Westminster, 1954), pp. 115–28.

[35]Cf. my essay in *Novum Testamentum* 12 (1970): 218–22.

[36]Cf. my book, *To Heal and to Reveal*, chaps. 1 and 2.

[37]Cf. my book, *Horizons of Christian Community* (St. Louis: Bethany, 1959), pp. 26–37.

[38]See Ricoeur, *Conflict*, p. 316.

[39]It may be observed that the same problems of interpreting symbolic language appear in connection with the Negro spiritual that utilizes the idiom of falling stars. The spiritual may be sufficient in catching certain nuances of Mark 13:24–27 where professional exegesis has been deficient.

> *My Lord, what a morning! My Lord, what a morning!*
>
> . . . .
>
> *You'll hear my Jesus come, To wake the nations underground,*
> *Look in my God's right hand, When de stars begin to fall.*

[40]See Kroner, *Culture and Faith*, p. 271.

[41]See *Works of Love* (Princeton: Princeton University, 1946), pp. 182–213.

[42]Here again Kierkegaard, in his *Gospel of Suffering*, discusses a neglected dimension of New Testament thought.

[43]Scholars have long been accustomed to characterize Hellenic attitudes toward time as cyclical and biblical attitudes as linear. I suggest that it is more accurate to characterize biblical attitudes as *vocational*. It is God's calling of his people which provides biblical thinking about time with its distinctive sense of motivation, momenta, directions, crises, origins, and consummations. In a fashion this whole book is an explication of this vocational orientation of time.

Index of Biblical References